Get Off the Sidelines

and

Into the "Game"

—◦◦◦—

Quotes to Inspire a
Game Plan for Successful Living

—◦◦◦—

By

Dr. Deborah J. Hrivnak

America's #1 Action Coach

RockStar
PUBLISHING HOUSE

Published by
RockStar Publishing House
32129 Lindero Canyon Road, Suite 205
Westlake Village, CA 91361
www.rockstarpublishinghouse.com

Manufactured in the United States of America,
or in the United Kingdom when distributed elsewhere.

Author Hrivnak, Deborah
Title of Book: Get Off the Sidelines and Into the Game
ISBN:
Paperback: 9781937506919
eBook: 9781937506926

Cover design by: Tim Durning, Scribe Inc.
Cover photo by: Val and Stephanie Westover
Interior design: Jason Hughes, Scribe Inc.
Photo credits: Val and Stephanie Westover

www.MyCoachDeborah.com

Contents

Dedication

I dedicate this book to my amazing grandchildren.
There is no greater joy than to experience the love of
a grandchild. I am truly blessed . . .

—◈◈◈—

Jaydin, Jancye, and Jenna

Reagan, Beckett, and Kennedy

Anna and Isaac

Declan and Gilbert

—◈◈◈—

Acknowledgements

—◦◦◦—

I am most grateful to God for this incredible journey
and the many opportunities and challenges along
the way! "Success is never so interesting as struggle."

WILLA CATHER

I would like to extend my deepest appreciation to my
sons and daughter-in-laws—Justin and Jaime, Chace and
Kelli. You inspire everything that I do. You are truly a gift
from God.

To my stepchildren—David and Nancy, Daniel and Tif-
fany, Andrew and Melanie, and Stephen, thank you for the
many gifts you have given me simply by knowing you.

Susie McCowen, Pat Nosal, and Lore Raymond—you per-
sonify the true definition of "friend." To my parents—Jack
and Betty Anderson, thank you for putting me on this journey and acknowledging my accomplishments along the way.

Many individuals have inspired me throughout the years
and impact my life in many ways—Pat Abinion, Lisa Anderson, Ken Arndt, Teresa Barnes, Jennifer Bricker, Sue Brooke,
Larry Broughton, Kim Brown, Les Brown, Ron Brown, Warren

Buffet, Bob Burg, Valerie Brunnberg, Brendon Bruchard, Dean Cain, Luke Cano, Karen Carlson, Sandra Champlain, Donald Clifton, Meg Cole, Lorry Cook, Carol Costello, Julie Cullen, Melanie Denney, Bob Devaney, Joe Dichiara, Joanne Dowdell, Craig and Natasha Duswalt and the entire RockStar Marketing community, Maryann and Eugene Ehmann, Hilde Elg, Audra Erwin, Eldonna Fernandez, Heather Ford, Linda Fowlkes, Patricia Gagic, Katrina Garcia, Jane Gerold, Eleanor Gilski, Randy Gold, Denise Gorlich, Walt Grassl, Bruce and Lorraine Green, Richard Grieger, Sandra Hanesworth, Bill Hickey, Ernie Hudson, Donna Hultman, Arnie Klehm, Linda Kobusz-Kosan, Penny Kowal, Loral Langemeier, Cynthia Lay, JoAnne Lefelstein, Judith Lefeber, Janie Lidey, Robert McKanna, Sharon McNeely, James Malinchak, William Malinchak, Paul Mata, Nancy Matthews, Karen Montgomery, Glenn Morshower, Linda Mueller, Charlene and Dave Nassaney, Jim Nicodem, Dennis O'Malley, Tom Osborne, Toni Palan, Cindy Pauer, Jay Payleitner, Carol Pilkington, Ricky Powell, Christopher Rausch, Nicole Rhoades, Forbes Riley, Tony Robbins, Jim Rohn, Rudy Ruetliger, Miguel Sanchez, Kristen Sharma, Susan Shepherd, Robert Sidell, Carol Shockley, Marcus Slaton, Andy Sokol, Gina St. George, Karen Strauss, Joe Sugarman, Jamie Teasdale, Yoti Telio, Joe Theismann, Louise and Sid Tiemann, Murray Thompson, Sara Thompson, Brian Tracy, Christine Welch, Sally Van Swearingen, Val and Stephanie Westover, Mike Wolf, Laura Wormsley, and Dorothy Young.

Most importantly, I wish to express my love and appreciation to my husband and best friend, John. Thank you for keeping me on task with your occasional inquiry as to whether I had completed writing a chapter or not, and for taking on additional responsibilities that allowed more time in my schedule to write. It is because of your ongoing prayer support, encouragement, and love that this book was completed. I am forever grateful to be doing life with you. WGATAP!

Introduction

—◦◦◦—

Congratulations! By picking up this book, you have already taken action to get off the sidelines and into the game. Everybody loves quotes, and whether you read this book for your personal or professional use, you will find these words of wisdom inspiring and empowering.

Get Off the Sidelines and Into the "Game" is inspired by my love for football and for life. Growing up in Nebraska, football is more than a sport. It is about core values that include hard work, family, and community. Individuals come together to connect and build community with a sense of pride and recognition. In any sport, each individual must work hard, be dedicated to the sport, and sometimes spend years preparing and waiting for the opportunity to make a game-changing difference. Such is also true in life, if we want to excel in any area.

Everyone has the opportunity to define for himself or herself what success means. I have found, in my experience, that all successful people want to contribute to others. They learn that their success took a team and the support of others to reach their goals. Never giving up, living with integrity and gratitude, and walking in faith are important factors when leaving a legacy that reflects our authentic selves.

We often see people who stand on the sidelines, not participating fully in the game of life. Even successful people miss huge opportunities for even more success. We may decide not to take action when these opportunities arise due to our negative mind-set, fear of failure, or fear of success. Some allow complaining, criticizing, uncertainty, and unwillingness to get in the way of being the successes they are.

When you see opportunities, take action, and have clarity, commitment, and confidence. Vision and purpose can help you make decisions leading to further success. Ongoing preparation, maintaining good health, resilience, passion, and being coachable are just a few areas on which we must focus to be in the game.

What effect has inaction had on your life? We all love watching others succeed—especially in sports—and everyone loves inspirational stories when others have had a tremendous impact on others in some way. Are there obstacles or challenges that are getting in the way of your success? Are you ready to fully participate in this game we call life?

It is your time to take action and get off the sidelines and into the game. Create a personal game plan—a plan that will be a game changer for you! May this book, *Get Off the Sidelines and Into the "Game,"* inspire you to take action! Be who it is you came here to be! I want to celebrate your success—let me know how your personal "game" has improved from the inspiration in this book.

What Others Are Saying

—⦂〰⦂—

As a seasoned entrepreneur, I know some of the challenges that face businesspeople. Quite often, we hit roadblocks, lose our clarity, and simply don't feel motivated. This book is filled with great quotes that will inspire, motivate, and help you get back on your game. Deborah has chosen some amazing quotes from some of the greatest thought leaders of our time and put them all in one place. I think this book should be on every entrepreneur's shelf.

> —MIKE WOLF, "The Homeless Millionaire" serial
> entrepreneur and founder of
> MikeWolfMastery.com and
> Freedom Lifestyle Entrepreneurs

Dr. Deborah Hrivnak has hit it out of the park with *Get Off the Sidelines and Into the "Game"*! This is a powerful collection of quotes that will inspire you throughout your life. Whether you're looking for a little pick me up or advice to share with a friend, this book has it all.

> —NANCY MATTHEWS, speaker, author of *The One
> Philosophy*, and founder of Women's Prosperity Network

There are not enough positive adjectives to describe Deborah Hrivnak! She exudes excellence extraordinaire in her craft as a coach and educator, a been-there, done-that authenticity, a get-it-done energy, all wrapped up in a big bear hug and a heart-warming smile. Knowing the power of resiliency and having to redefine herself, she can help anyone journey through transition and get the results they truly desire.

—MARYANN EHMANN, author of *Create Your Magnificent Life Now*, speaker, and coach, maryannehmann.com

Deborah takes us on a journey through the shadows and windows of our mind. With her eloquent and deep sharing, we become more aware of our inner qualities and opportunities. Deborah makes us realize how precious our minds are and how wisdom is there for the taking! This book is an absolute must for all who venture into the world of the creative, academic, and curious. What a special treat to feel her powerful coaching allowing us to share the inspirational and evolutionary gifts! This book will long be heralded as a "keeper" and one that everyone will reference for many years in the future!

—PATRICIA KAREN GAGIC, Dame Commander, Order of St. George; international artist; and author of *Karmic Alibi*

Dr. Hrivnak has done all of us a great service. If you are human, you are going to need to be encouraged, consoled, coached, and challenged. Inside this marvelous book, you will find words and ideas that do all those things and more.

—JAY PAYLEITNER, bestselling author of 15 books, including *The Dad Book* and *What If God Wrote Your Bucket List*

Everyone likes games . . . and football is one of America's favorites. The analogy of a game plan applies to life in general, and it is easy to see the application. Dr. Deborah Hrivnak has captured an abundance of wisdom on these pages for you and your life. Don't just read through it, but let yourself digest it in snippets.

—KAREN M. CARLSON, contributing author of *Strengthen Your Wings* and national energy consultant, Team LTD

PART I

Success

———∙∿∙———

*T*he closer one gets to the top, the more one finds there is no "top."

NANCY BARCUS

*I*f you really look closely, most overnight successes took a long time.

STEVE JOBS

*S*uccess is a lousy teacher. It seduces smart people into thinking they can't lose.

BILL GATES

*T*he difference between successful people and really successful people is that really successful people say no to almost everything.

WARREN BUFFETT

S uccess is the result of perfection, hard work, learning from failure, loyalty, and persistence.

COLIN POWELL

W hen a man feels throbbing within him, the power to do what he undertakes as well as it can possibly be done, this is happiness, this is success.

ORISON SWETT MARDEN

S uccess is falling nine times and getting up ten.

JON BON JOVI

S uccess is doing ordinary things extraordinarily well.

JIM ROHN

I want to define success by redefining it. For me it isn't that solely mythical definition—glamour, allure, power of wealth, and the privilege from care. Any definition of success should be personal because it's so transitory. It's about shaping my own destiny.

ANITA RODDICK

W hat is success? I think it is a mixture of having a flair for the thing that you are doing; knowing that it is not enough, that you have got to have hard work and a certain sense of purpose.

MARGARET THATCHER

*S*uccess is how high you bounce when you hit bottom.

GEORGE S. PATTON

*S*uccess is not the key to happiness. Happiness is the key to success.

ALBERT SCHWEITZER

*P*atience, persistence and perspiration make an unbeatable combination for success.

NAPOLEON HILL

*T*o succeed in life, you need two things: ignorance and confidence.

MARK TWAIN

*A*lways bear in mind that your own resolution to succeed is more important than any other one thing.

ABRAHAM LINCOLN

*S*uccess in life could be defined as the continued expansion of happiness and the progressive realization of worthy goals.

DEEPAK CHOPRA

I've failed over and over and over again in my life and that is why I succeed.

MICHAEL JORDAN

Success is not forever and failure isn't fatal.

DON SHULA

I know of no single formula for success, but over the years I have observed that some attributes of leadership are universal, and are often about finding ways of encouraging people to combine their efforts, their talents, their insights, their enthusiasm and their inspiration, to work together.

QUEEN ELIZABETH II

Real success is finding your lifework in the work that you love.

DAVID MCCULLOUGH

Don't aim for success if you want it; just do what you love and believe in, and it will come naturally.

DAVID FROST

Success and failure. We think of them as opposites, but they're really not. They're companions—the hero and the sidekick.

LAURENCE SHAMES

PART II

Pregame

———⟨∿⟩———

Adversity

When adversity strikes—and it will—I think we have three choices. The first is to quit. The second is to blame someone else. The third is to learn from the experience.

DR. TOM OSBORNE

A successful man is one who can lay a firm foundation with the bricks others have thrown at him.

DAVID BRINKLEY

There's no reason why you can't . . . be whatever you want to be. Do whatever you want to do. Be whoever you want to be. Stop making excuses. Get off your butt and make it happen because nothing will happen unless you make it happen.

SUE BROOKE

*E*xpect trouble as an inevitable part of life, and when it comes, hold your head high, look it squarely in the eye, and say "I will be bigger than you. You cannot defeat me."

ANN LANDERS

*N*early all men can stand adversity, but if you want to test a man's character, give him power.

ABRAHAM LINCOLN

*Y*ou may encounter many defeats, but you must not be defeated. In fact, it may be necessary to encounter the defeats, so you can know who you are, what you can rise from, how you can still come out of it.

MAYA ANGELOU

*N*ever to suffer would never to have been blessed.

EDGAR ALLAN POE

*I*t isn't as bad as you sometimes think it is. It all works out. Don't worry. I say that to myself every morning. It all works out in the end. Put your trust in God, and move forward with faith and confidence in the future. The Lord will not forsake us. He will not forsake us. If we will put our trust in Him, if we will pray to Him, if we will live worthy of His blessings, He will hear our prayers.

GORDON B. HINCKLEY

*Y*ou will face your greatest opposition when you are closest to your biggest miracle.

SHANNON L. ALDER

*B*reakdowns can create breakthroughs. Things fall apart so things can fall together.

UNKNOWN

*L*ife is a series of experiences, each one of which makes us bigger, even though sometimes it is hard to realize this. For the world was built to develop character, and we must learn that the setbacks and grieves which we endure help us in our marching onward.

HENRY FORD

Assumptions

*I*f the shoe fits, it's probably your size.

UNKNOWN

*W*e simply assume that the way we see things is the way they really are or the way they should be. And our attitudes and behaviors grow out of these assumptions.

STEPHEN COVEY

*D*on't make assumptions. Find the courage to ask questions and to express what you really want. Communicate with others as clearly as you can to avoid misunderstandings, sadness and drama. With just this one agreement, you can completely transform your life.

MIGUEL ÁNGEL RUIZ

*Y*ou must stick to your conviction, but be ready to abandon your assumptions.

DENIS WAITLEY

*E*uclid taught me that without assumptions there is no proof. Therefore, in any argument, examine the assumptions.

E. T. BELL

I have also found that by making four simple assumptions in our lives we can immediately begin leading a more balanced, integrated, powerful life. They are simple—one for each part of our nature—but I promise you that if you do them consistently, you will find a new wellspring of strength and integrity to draw on when you need it most.

1) For the *body*—assume you've had a heart attack; now live accordingly.

2) For the *mind*—assume the half-life of your profession is two years; now prepare accordingly.

3) For the *heart*—assume everything you say about another, they can overhear; now speak accordingly.

4) For the *spirit*—assume you have a one-on-one visit with your Creator every quarter; now live accordingly.

STEPHEN COVEY

I have learned as a composer chiefly through my mistakes and pursuits of false assumptions, not by my exposure to fonts of wisdom and knowledge.

IGOR STRAVINSKY

*I*f you're interested in misery, 1) always try to look good in front of others; 2) always live in a world of assumptions and treat each assumption as though it's a reality; 3) relate to every new situation as if it is a small crisis; 4) always live in the future or the past; and 5) occasionally stomp on yourself for being so dumb as to follow the first four rules.

W. W. BROADBENT

*N*ever assume, seldom deny, always distinguish.

UNKNOWN

*B*y and large, I seem to have made more mistakes than any others of whom I know, but have learned thereby to make ever swifter acknowledgment of the errors and thereafter immediately set about to deal more effectively with the truths disclosed by the acknowledgment of erroneous assumptions.

R. BUCKMINSTER FULLER

*T*here is no sound basis upon which it may be assumed that all poor men are godly and all rich men are evil, no more than it could be assumed that all rich men are good and all poor men are bad.

NORMAN VINCENT PEALE

Challenges

*D*on't limit your challenges; challenge your limits.

JERRY DUNN

*Y*ou know, if you're a human and living on the planet, it doesn't matter what you do; you are not immune to the challenges, the trials, the difficulty. And that fact that I happen to be a coach and a minister and a spiritual teacher doesn't mean anything. I'm still human.

IYANLA VANZANT

*L*arry's short list for doing better: Stop complaining about your results. (No one really cares, anyway.) Whining about the problem only prolongs the problem. Take a realistic look at your results and think about what you have done or not done in the past that contributed to them. Go to the closest mirror, look yourself in the eye, and say, "This is all my fault." Take responsibility. Do a reality check and admit that change has been going on for a good long while and you survived. You will survive this, too. Make a list of what you are going to do differently in the future to change your results. Doing better is the result of deciding to do better and then taking action on that decision.

LARRY WINGET

Sometimes, struggles are exactly what we need in our life. If we were to go through our life without any obstacles, we would be crippled. We would not be as strong as what we could have been. Give every opportunity a chance, leave no room for regrets.

FRIEDRICH NIETZSCHE

Character cannot be developed in ease and quiet. Only through experience of trial and suffering can the soul be strengthened, vision cleared, ambition inspired, and success achieved.

HELEN KELLER

The search is no overnight affair. It is a progression of steps, measured in tiny increments of success, in an endless journey of challenge and discovery.

DR. JOSEF KNIPP

We have discovered that life is an exciting journey, so you really have only two options on this road called life, either choose to enjoy the journey, or decide to be miserable.

CHARLENE AND DAVID NASSANEY

Life is a gift and a challenge.

JAY PAYLEITNER

If you aren't in over your head, how do you know how tall you are?

T. S. ELIOT

*T*hose who overcome great challenges will be changed, and often in unexpected ways. For our struggles enter our lives as unwelcome guests, but they bring valuable gifts. And once the pain subsides, the gifts remain. These gifts are life's true treasures, bought at great price, but cannot be acquired in any other way.

STEVE GOODIER

*T*hings turn out best for those who make the best out of the way things turn out.

JOHN WOODEN

Complaining

*N*ow I get that complaining just feels good. And, when you're upset about something, it's good to get it out of your system. The key here is to complain to the right person. Either the person who has authority to change the situation, or someone who will allow you to vent but not travel down the rabbit hole with you.

NANCY MATTHEWS

*T*he man who complains about the way the ball bounces is likely the one who dropped it.

LOU HOLTZ

*C*onstant complaint is the poorest sort of pay for all the comforts we enjoy.

BENJAMIN FRANKLIN

*I*f I were to say, "God, why me?" about the bad things, then I should have said, "God, why me?" about the good things that happened in my life.

ARTHUR ASHE

*I*f you don't like how things are, change it! You're not a tree.

JIM ROHN

*W*hat we need to do is always lean into the future; when the world changes around you and when it changes against you—what used to be a tail wind is now a head wind—you have to lean into that and figure out what to do because complaining isn't a strategy.

JEFF BEZOS

*W*atch out for the joy-stealers: gossip, criticism, complaining, faultfinding, and a negative, judgmental attitude.

JOYCE MEYER

*W*hen a person finds themselves predisposed to complaining about how little they are regarded by others, let them reflect how little they have contributed to the happiness of others.

SAMUEL JOHNSON

*I*f you have time to whine and complain about something then you have the time to do something about it.

ANTHONY J. D'ANGELO

A pessimist is somebody who complains about the noise when opportunity knocks.

OSCAR WILDE

*C*omplaining is a complete waste of one's energy. Those who complain the most accomplish the least.

ROBERT TEW

Criticizing

*B*ack in the 1930s, Carl Jung, the eminent thinker and psychologist, put it this way: Criticism has "the power to do good when there is something that must be destroyed, dissolved or reduced, but [it is] capable only of harm when there is something to be built."

DONALD O. CLIFTON

*W*hen we judge or criticize another person, it says nothing about that person; it merely says something about our own need to be critical.

UNKNOWN

*C*riticism is an indirect form of self-boasting.

EMMET FOX

I had three rules for my players: No profanity. Don't criticize a teammate. Never be late.

JOHN WOODEN

*C*riticism of others is futile and if you indulge in it often you should be warned that it can be fatal to your career.

DALE CARNEGIE

*L*et the refining and improving of your own life keep you so busy that you have little time to criticize others.

H. JACKSON BROWN JR.

*A*ll of us could take a lesson from the weather. It pays no attention to criticism.

UNKNOWN

*D*on't criticize what you can't understand.

BOB DYLAN

*A*ny fool can criticize, condemn and complain— and most fools do.

BENJAMIN FRANKLIN

*B*e an encourager. The world has plenty of critics already.

DAVE WILLIS

*D*o not criticize!

UNKNOWN

Difficult People

*T*he world, and therefore the workplace, is full of idiots. And the reality of life is that when you get rid of one idiot, another will show up to take his place. It's the curse of humanity.

LARRY WINGET

*L*etting the wrong people hang around is unfair to all the right people, as they inevitably find themselves compensating for the inadequacies of the wrong people. Worse, it can drive away the best people. Strong performers are intrinsically motivated by performance, and when they see their efforts impeded by carrying extra weight, they eventually become frustrated.

JAMES C. COLLINS

*S*ometimes a neighbor whom we have disliked a lifetime for his arrogance and conceit lets fall a single commonplace remark that shows us another side, another man, really; a man uncertain, and puzzled, and in the dark like ourselves.

WILLA CATHER

*L*et go of people who dull your shine, poison your spirit, and bring you drama. Cancel your subscription to their issues.

DR. STEVE MARABOLI

I didn't respond well to a firm hand and insults.

TERRY BRADSHAW

*B*efore accepting the negative chatter that you aren't good enough, smart enough, tall enough, small enough, strong enough, rich enough, or whatever enough; first, be sure you aren't surrounded by jerks, pin heads, scaredy cats, drama queens, or imbeciles.

LARRY BROUGHTON

*Y*ou can't tell stories and really walk in someone's shoes and not have a love for them, even if they're doing horrible things.

SHONDA RHIMES

*W*e are constantly being put to the test by trying circumstances and difficult people and problems not necessarily of our own making.

TERRY BROOKS

I don't have to attend every argument I'm invited to.

UNKNOWN

Some people won't be happy until they've pushed you to the ground. What you have to do is have the courage to stand your ground and not give them the time of day. Hold on to your power and never give it away.

DONNA SCHOENROCK

If two men on a job agree all the time, then one is useless. If they disagree all the time, then both are useless.

DARRYL F. ZANUCK

Failure

A champion is afraid of losing. Everyone else is afraid of winning.

BILLIE JEAN KING

It is impossible to live without failing at something, unless you live so cautiously that you might as well not have lived at all—in which case, you fail by default.

J. K. ROWLING

I have not failed. I've just found 10,000 ways that won't work.

THOMAS EDISON

*I*n high school, in sport, I had a coach who told me I was much better than I thought I was, and would make me do more in a positive sense. He was the first person who taught me not to be afraid of failure.

MIKE KRZYZEWSKI

*W*ould you like me to give you a formula for success? It's quite simple, really. Double your rate of failure. You are thinking of failure as the enemy of success. But it isn't at all. You can be discouraged by failure—or you can learn from it. So go ahead and make mistakes. Make all you can. Because, remember, that's where you will find success.

THOMAS J. WATSON

*S*uccess is going from failure to failure without losing your enthusiasm.

ABRAHAM LINCOLN

I've never had a failure in my life . . . just educational experiences that didn't go my way.

JOE THEISMANN

*N*ot many people are willing to give failure a second opportunity. They fail once and it is all over. The bitter pill of failure is often more than most people can handle. If you are willing to accept failure and learn from it, if you are willing to consider failure as a blessing in disguise and bounce back, you have got the essential of harnessing one of the most powerful success forces.

JOSEPH SUGARMAN

*S*uccess represents the 1% of your work which results from the 99% that is called failure.

SOICHIRO HONDA

*I*n the business world today, failure is apparently not an option. We need to change this attitude toward failure—and celebrate the idea that only by falling on our collective business faces do we learn enough to succeed down the road.

NAVEEN JAIN

*W*hen we build on our strengths and daily successes—instead of focusing on failures—we simply learn more.

TOM RATH

Fear

A bird sitting on a tree is never afraid of the branch breaking, because its trust is not on the branch but on its own wings. Always believe in yourself.

YOTI TELIO

*N*inety-nine percent of people believe they can't do great things, so they aim for mediocrity.

TIM FERRISS

You can't live in fear. Live in such a way that you're always celebrating life. Wake up every day happy, knowing you're the best that you can be. If you can banish fear, you'll rest easy, knowing that you can handle anything you come up against. When an athlete succeeds, everybody cheers. So why not do that for yourself? You kiss a pretty girl? Cheers. You landed a commission at work? Cheer for yourself.

BRUCE BUFFER

Fear paints a picture that communicates an end that is different from the future that I have promised you.

CAROL SHOCKLEY

The cave you fear to enter holds the treasure you seek.

JOSEPH CAMPBELL

Pain means you're growing. Fear means you are risking. Tears mean it mattered. Take what hurts you and let it help you.

MANDY HALE

We would accomplish many more things if we did not think of them as impossible.

VINCE LOMBARDI

There is no living thing that is not afraid when it faces danger. The true courage is in facing danger when you are afraid, and that kind of courage you have in plenty.

L. FRANK BAUM

Fear is not a word in my football dictionary.

JOSÉ MOURINHO

We can easily forgive a child who is afraid of the dark; the real tragedy of life is when men are afraid of the light.

UNKNOWN

The oldest and strongest emotion of mankind is fear, and the oldest and strongest kind of fear is fear of the unknown.

H. P. LOVECRAFT

Forgiveness

Forgive yourself for your faults and your mistakes and move on.

LES BROWN

Forgiveness should be extended to all people who have touched our lives. For we know not what their destiny is, their reason for being. At the same time we should grant to ourselves the same dispensation of forgiveness, continually and liberally.

ROBERT SIDELL

*T*o forgive is to set a prisoner free and discover that the prisoner was you.

LEWIS B. SMEDES

I learned a long time ago that some people would rather die than forgive. It's a strange truth, but forgiveness is a painful and difficult process. It's not something that happens overnight. It's an evolution of the heart.

SUE MONK KIDD

*T*he stupid neither forgive nor forget; the naive forgive and forget; the wise forgive but do not forget.

THOMAS SZASZ

*I*nner peace can be reached only when we practice forgiveness. Forgiveness is letting go of the past, and is therefore the means for correcting our misperceptions.

GERALD JAMPOLSKY

*W*hen you forgive, you in no way change the past—but you sure do change the future.

BERNARD MELTZER

*T*o err is human; to forgive, divine.

ALEXANDER POPE

*F*orgive yourself for your faults and your mistakes and move on.

LES BROWN

I can forgive, but I cannot forget, is only another way of saying, I will not forgive. Forgiveness ought to be like a cancelled note—torn in two, and burned up, so that it never can be shown against one.

HENRY WARD BEECHER

A winner rebukes and forgives; a loser is too timid to rebuke and too petty to forgive.

SYDNEY J. HARRIS

Letting Go

*T*he day came when the risk to remain tight in a bud was more painful than the risk it took to blossom.

ANAÏS NIN

*L*etting go means to come to the realization that some people are a part of your history, but not a part of your destiny.

DR. STEVE MARABOLI

*M*any people have sighed for the "good old days" and regretted the "passing of the horse," but today, when only those who like horses own them, it is a far better time for horses.

C. W. ANDERSON

*L*etting go doesn't mean that you don't care about someone anymore. It's just realizing that the only person you really have control over is yourself.

DEBORAH REBER

*Y*ou will find that it is necessary to let things go; simply for the reason that they are heavy. So let them go, let go of them. I tie no weights to my ankles.

C. JOYBELL C.

*S*ome people believe holding on and hanging in there are signs of great strength. However, there are times when it takes much more strength to know when to let go and then do it.

ANN LANDERS

*T*here are times in life when people must know when not to let go. Balloons are designed to teach small children this.

TERRY PRATCHETT

I realize there's something incredibly honest about trees in winter, how they're experts at letting things go.

JEFFREY MCDANIEL

*T*oday expect something good to happen to you no matter what occurred yesterday. Realize the past no longer holds you captive. It can only continue to hurt you if you hold on to it. Let the past go. A simply abundant world awaits.

SARAH BAN BREATHNACH

*A*ll the art of living lies in a fine mingling of letting go and holding on.

HENRY HAVELOCK ELLIS

*D*etachment means letting go and nonattachment means simply letting be.

STEPHEN LEVINE

Mistakes

*S*uccess does not consist in never making mistakes but in never making the same one a second time.

GEORGE BERNARD SHAW

I've learned that something constructive comes from every defeat.

TOM LANDRY

*E*ven if you fall on your face, you're still moving forward.

VICTOR KIAM

*W*hat do you do with a mistake: recognize it, admit it, learn from it, forget it.

DEAN SMITH

*T*he biggest mistake you could ever make is being too afraid to make one.

UNKNOWN

*W*e don't make mistakes, just happy little accidents.

BOB ROSS

*Y*ou miss 100% of the shots you don't take.

WAYNE GRETZKY

*A*n error doesn't become a mistake until you refuse to correct it.

ORLANDO A. BATTISTA

*M*istakes are the portals of discovery.

JAMES JOYCE

A life spent making mistakes is not only more honorable, but more useful than a life spent doing nothing.

GEORGE BERNARD SHAW

I think making mistakes and discovering them for yourself is of great value, but to have someone else to point out your mistakes is a shortcut of the process.

SHELBY FOOTE

Negativity

*Y*ou can't live a positive life with a negative mind.

DIANE CARDEN

*T*ackle the difficult things first in the morning; make changes in the way you network. Treat everyone with respect and dignity. This stops you from cynicism and negativity. End your day with that same attitude you started. Renew your contract with a day well completed.

RICK PITINO

*I*gnoring negative things that need to be changed is destructive and does nothing to alleviate negativity. Instead, we should focus on the way we're treating other people in our brief interactions with them.

TOM RATH

*N*egativity is the enemy of creativity.

DAVID LYNCH

*P*rotect your enthusiasm from the negativity of others.

H. JACKSON BROWN JR.

*N*obody can motivate himself in a positive direction by continually using negative words.

JOHN C. MAXWELL

*B*elieving in negative thoughts is the single greatest obstruction to success.

CHARLES F. GLASSMAN

*T*he more you talk about negative things in your life, the more you call them in. Speak victory not defeat.

JOEL OSTEEN

*I*f you accept the expectations of others, especially negative ones, then you never will change the outcome.

MICHAEL JORDAN

*S*ome people grumble that roses have thorns; I am grateful that thorns have roses.

ALPHONSE KARR

*W*hether you think you can, or you think you can't, either way you're right.

HENRY FORD

Obstacles

You are the sum of the obstacles you overcome.

FORBES RILEY

You're never a loser until you quit trying.

MIKE DITKA

God places the heaviest burden on those who can carry its weight.

REGGIE WHITE

If you're trying to achieve, there will be roadblocks. I've had them; everybody has had them. But obstacles don't have to stop you. If you run into a wall, don't turn around and give up. Figure out how to climb it, go through it, or work around it.

MICHAEL JORDAN

I've always found that anything worth achieving will always have obstacles in the way and you've got to have that drive and determination to overcome those obstacles on route to whatever it is that you want to accomplish.

CHUCK NORRIS

Obstacles are those frightful things you see when you take your eyes off your goal.

HENRY FORD

A man does what he must—in spite of personal consequences, in spite of obstacles and dangers, and pressures—and that is the basis of all human morality.

JOHN F. KENNEDY

I think a hero is an ordinary individual who finds strength to persevere and endure in spite of over-whelming obstacles.

CHRISTOPHER REEVE

S tand up to your obstacles and do something about them. You will find that they haven't half the strength you think they have.

NORMAN VINCENT PEALE

O ne who gains strength by overcoming obstacles possesses the only strength which can overcome adversity.

ALBERT SCHWEITZER

S ome minds seem almost to create themselves, springing up under every disadvantage, and work-ing their solitary but irresistible way through a thou-sand obstacles.

WASHINGTON IRVING

Perfection

*P*erfectionists do not like surrendering or making mistakes. They don't like failing, because that's not perfect, or good enough, and they are conditioned to be so. In these cases, obstacles are avoided or denied, rather than confronted. Since every path to anything worthwhile has obstacles, perfectionists do not pursue these paths.

LORAL LANGEMEIER

*T*o be completely perfect, to need no more training or coaching, is to stagnate or die—and in many cases, to be dismissed. To know everything is to be un . . . believable.

SAM PARKER

*P*erfectionism is an endless path.

CAROL PILKINGTON

*P*erfection is not attainable, but if we chase perfection, we can catch excellence.

VINCE LOMBARDI

*S*trive for continuous improvement, instead of perfection.

KIM COLLINS

*N*o one is perfect . . . that's why pencils have erasers.

WOLFGANG RIEBE

*D*on't let the seeds stop you from enjoying the watermelon.

SETH GODEN

*L*ife does not have to be perfect to be wonderful.

ANNETTE FUNICELLO

*T*he pursuit of excellence is gratifying and heathy, the pursuit of perfection is frustrating, neurotic, and a terrible waste of time.

EDWIN BLISS

*S*tart where you are. Use what you have. Do what you can.

ARTHUR ASHE

I'm not saying I'm perfect; in fact I'm far from it; I'm just saying I'm worth it.

UNKNOWN

Setbacks

*D*on't let a perceived setback hold you back.

JOE THEISMANN

*B*ottom line is, if you turn the ball over to a team that isn't as good, you then have brought them up to your level.

TERRY BRADSHAW

*I*n times like these, it helps to recall that there have always been times like these.

PAUL HARVEY

*Y*ou hear about how many fourth quarter comebacks that a guy has and I think it means a guy screwed up in the first three quarters.

PEYTON MANNING

*T*he real glory is being knocked to your knees and then coming back. That's real glory. That's the essence of it.

VINCE LOMBARDI

*C*ultivate optimism by committing yourself to a cause, a plan or a value system. You'll feel that you are growing in a meaningful direction which will help you rise above day-to-day setbacks.

DR. ROBERT CONROY

*M*ost of the important things in the world have been accomplished by people who have kept on trying when there seemed to be no hope at all.

DALE CARNEGIE

I'm proud of the way I've dealt with setbacks. It's hard when you feel down and you think, "Why is the world doing this to me?" But you have to pick yourself up again. That's what makes you a better athlete.

JESSICA ENNIS

*F*ailure? I never encountered it. All I ever met were temporary setbacks.

DOTTIE WALTERS

*W*ho I am today is what experience, obstacles and setbacks I have gone through, without them I wouldn't be as effective a leader I am today.

CHRISTOPHER CHAN

*N*ever give up. Keep your thoughts and your mind always on the goal. One of the secrets of success is to refuse to let temporary setbacks defeat you.

UNKNOWN

Time

*T*ime is like a vacuum cleaner; it gifts you with a tool to clean up a mess, but once it inhales there is no place to hide; it still exists, but in a different form. It is now out of sight and yet always in existence.

PATRICIA GAGIC

*I*n every day, there are 1,440 minutes. That means we have 1,440 daily opportunities to make a positive impact.

LES BROWN

*T*ime you enjoy wasting is not wasted time.

MARTHE TROLY-CURTIN

*R*egret for wasted time is more wasted time.

MASON COOLEY

*I*n the landscape of time, there are few locations less comfortable than that of one who waits for some person or event to arrive at some unknown moment in the future.

ROBERT GRUDIN

*T*he present time has one advantage over every other—it is our own.

CHARLES CALEB COLTON

*T*here is never enough time to do everything, but there is always enough time to do the most important thing.

BRIAN TRACY

*T*ime is the coin of your life. It is the only coin you have, and only you can determine how it will be spent. Be careful lest you let other people spend it for you.

CARL SANDBURG

*H*ow did it get so late so soon? It's night before it's afternoon. December is here before it's June. My goodness how the time has flewn. How did it get so late so soon?

DR. SEUSS

*I*t's being here now that's important. There's no past and there's no future. Time is a very misleading thing. All there is ever, is the now. We can gain experience from the past, but we can't relive it; and we can hope for the future, but we don't know if there is one.

GEORGE HARRISON

*E*verything happens to everybody sooner or later if there is time enough.

GEORGE BERNARD SHAW

Uncertainty

*Y*ou know that uncertainty you feel today? It never goes away. The question is, do you know how to make uncertainty your friend?

DAVID BROOKS

*Y*ou must be able to let go of the past, whatever success you may have seen, whatever your comfort, whatever your habits. To me, that's the key to loving life: Enabling yourself to step bravely into the unknown. Only there will you find yourself again.

JULIETTE BINOCHES

*I*f you aren't in the moment, you are either looking forward to uncertainty, or back to pain and regret.

JIM CARREY

*E*xploring the unknown requires tolerating uncertainty.

BRIAN GREENE

*U*ncertainty and expectation are the joys of life. Security is an insipid thing.

WILLIAM CONGREVE

*C*hange is always tough. Even for those who see themselves as agents of change, the process of starting a new thing can cause times of disorientation, uncertainty and insecurity.

JOYCE MEYER

*A*lthough our intellect always longs for clarity and certainty, our nature often finds uncertainty fascinating.

CARL VON CLAUSEWITZ

*T*ruth is confirmed by inspection and delay; falsehood by haste and uncertainty.

TACITUS

I spent a lot of years trying to outrun or outsmart vulnerability by making things certain and definite, black and white, good and bad. My inability to lean into the discomfort of vulnerability limited the fullness of those important experiences that are wrought with uncertainty: Love, belonging, trust, joy, and creativity to name a few.

BRENÉ BROWN

*F*or my part I know nothing with any certainty, but the sight of the stars makes me dream.

VINCENT VAN GOGH

*U*ncertainty and mystery are energies of life. Don't let them scare you unduly, for they keep boredom at bay and spark creativity.

R. I. FITZHENRY

Uncomfortableness

*M*ove out of your comfort zone. You can only grow if you are willing to feel awkward and uncomfortable when you try something new.

BRIAN TRACY

I'm continually trying to make choices that put me against my own comfort zone. As long as you're uncomfortable, it means you're growing.

ASHTON KUTCHER

*W*e cannot become what we want to be by remaining what we are.

MAX DEPREE

*A*nything you to do to stretch yourself out of your comfort zone will ultimately enable you to take larger risks and grow.

LESLIE EVANS

*D*are to learn, to be different, to set your goals, to move out of your comfort zone, to be persistent.

UNKNOWN

A dream is your creative vision for your life in the future. You must break out of your current comfort zone and become comfortable with the unfamiliar and the unknown.

DENIS WAITLEY

*I*f you're in a comfort zone, afraid to venture out, / Remember that all winners were at one time filled with doubt.

UNKNOWN

*M*y experience is that you cannot have everything you want but you can have anything you really want, you just need to decide what it is and then plan your exit from the comfort zone.

JONATHAN FARRINGTON

*I*f you put yourself in a position where you have to stretch outside your comfort zone, then you are forced to expand your consciousness.

LES BROWN

A ship in harbor is safe, but that is not what ships are built for.

JOHN A. SHEDD

When you become comfortable with uncertainty, infinite possibilities open up in your life.

ECKHART TOLLE

Weaknesses

From the cradle to the cubicle, we devote more time to our shortcomings than to our strengths.

TOM RATH

From this point of view, to avoid your strengths and to focus on your weaknesses isn't a sign of diligent humility. It is almost irresponsible. By contrast the most responsible, the most challenging, and, in the sense of being true to yourself, the most honorable thing to do is face up to the strength potential inherent in your talents and then find ways to realize it.

DONALD O. CLIFTON

Our definition of a weakness is *anything that gets in the way of excellent performance.*

DONALD O. CLIFTON

Lean on each other's strengths; forgive each other's weaknesses.

UNKNOWN

The bigger your head, the easier to fill your shoes.

PHIL JACKSON

*B*e confident. Too many days are wasted comparing ourselves to others and wishing to be something we aren't. Everybody has their own strengths and weaknesses, and it is only when you accept everything that you are—and aren't—that you will truly succeed.

Unknown

*E*very one of us has our own strengths and weaknesses, and it is only when you accept everything you are, and aren't, that you will truly find the happiness and fulfillment you seek.

Melchor Lim

*S*top comparing yourself to other players. Everyone has their own strengths and weaknesses. You need all YOURS to reach your full potential.

Unknown

*B*uild upon strengths, and weaknesses will gradually take care of themselves.

Joyce C. Lock

*T*he chief executive who knows his strengths and weaknesses as a leader is likely to be far more effective than the one who remains blind to them.

John Adair

*B*uild on your strengths, work on your weaknesses.

Minh Tan

Worry

*W*orrying is like a rocking chair, it gives you something to do, but doesn't get you anywhere.

NATIONAL LAMPOON'S VAN WILDER

*W*orry never robs tomorrow of its sorrow, it only saps today of its joy.

LEO BUSCAGLIA

*D*on't worry about the horse being blind, just load the wagon.

JOHN MADDEN

*I*f only the people who worry about their liabilities would think about the riches they do possess, they would stop worrying.

DALE CARNEGIE

*D*on't worry about it. It's just a bunch of guys with an odd-shaped ball.

BILL PARCELLS

*N*ever worry about missing a field goal. Just blame the holder and think about making the next one.

LOU GROZA

*T*he only way to succeed is to not worry about what anyone else is doing.

Unknown

*W*hat's the use of worrying? / It never was worthwhile, so / Pack up your troubles in your old kit-bag, / And smile, smile, smile.

George Asaf

*W*orry does not empty tomorrow of its sorrow, it empties today of its strength.

Corrie ten Boom

*D*on't worry, be happy.

Bobby McFerrin

*I*f you want to gather honey, don't kick over the beehive.

Dale Carnegie

*D*on't worry, it will probably never happen.

Dr. Deborah J. Hrivnak

PART III

Game Time

—∿∿—

Accountability

*A*ccountability is the measure of a leaders height.
JEFFREY BENJAMIN

*Y*ou either make yourself accountable or you will be made accountable by your circumstances.
UNKNOWN

A body of men holding themselves accountable to nobody ought not to be trusted by anybody.
THOMAS PAINE

*L*ife is not accountable to us. We are accountable to life.
DENIS WAITLEY

*A*ccountability infers rules, responsibility infers caring.

DEAN SHARESKI

*I*t is not only what we do, but also what we do not do, for which we are accountable.

MOLIÈRE

*A*ccountability breeds response-ability.

STEPHEN COVEY

*T*rust, honesty, humility, transparency and accountability are the building blocks of a positive reputation. Trust is the foundation of any relationship.

MIKE PAUL

*A*ccountability separates the wishers in life from the action-takers that care enough about their future to account for their daily actions.

JOHN DI LEMME

*G*ood men are bound by conscience and liberated by accountability.

WES FESSLER

*W*hen it comes to privacy and accountability, people always demand the former for themselves and the latter for everyone else.

DAVID BRIN

Action

*D*o or do not. There is no try.

YODA

*D*on't wait until everything is just right. It will never be perfect. There will always be challenges, obstacles and less than perfect conditions. So what. Get started now. With each step you take, you will grow stronger and stronger, more and more skilled, more and more self-confident and more and more successful.

MARK VICTOR HANSEN

*T*ake the "T" out of can't!

JAMES MALINCHAK

A barking dog doesn't chase parked cars.

UNKNOWN

*H*aving just the vision's no solution, everything depends on execution.

STEPHEN SONDHEIM

I wish it was as simple as having a dream, closing our eyes, feeling good thoughts and the goal will come true. It is not. While all those things are part of achieving a goal, it is not all of it. You must take physical action to make the dream a reality. To take action, you first need a plan. Write out the goal and the things that would need to happen for that goal to be fulfilled. There will be action steps to take.

SANDRA CHAMPLAIN

*I*f you want to improve your life and the lives of those around you, you must take action.

TOM RATH

*N*o one has ever drowned in sweat.

LOU HOLTZ

*T*here are few secrets in football. So execute.

HANK STRAM

*R*emember, a real decision is measured by the fact that you've taken a new action. If there's no action, you haven't truly decided.

TONY ROBBINS

*A*ction is the foundational key to all success.

PABLO PICASSO

Adjustments

*I*f you don't like the road you're walking, start paving another.

DOLLY PARTON

A persistent attitude develops by staying the course instead of abandoning your goal when it becomes too challenging. However, persistence does not always mean staying with your original goal or decision. As important as it is to have a stick-with-it attitude, it is also wise to review your goals, decisions, and progress to make adjustments, which is often necessary.

KAREN CARLSON

*D*on't give up at half time. Concentrate on winning the second half.

PAUL BRYANT

*A*djustments, understanding and living the moment are recipe for having a good life.

UNKNOWN

*O*ne of the most difficult things everyone has to learn is that for your entire life you must keep fighting and adjusting if you hope to survive. No matter who you are or what your position is you must keep fighting for whatever it is you desire to achieve.

GEORGE ALLEN

*A*wesome people don't make excuses or blame others for their own failures, mistakes or letdowns. They stand by their decisions and make adjustments not excuses.

RICARDO HOUSHAM

*F*ailure does not lead to a dead end. I believe it leads to an opportunity to reflect on the aspects in your life that need adjustments or improvements.

UNKNOWN

*S*ome times you lose more than you win. It's about handling losses and trying to turn them into positives. You get out into the big leagues and there's a period of adjustment to be made. You've got to handle it.

LINDSAY DAVENPORT

*E*very new adjustment is a crisis in self-esteem.

ERIC HOFFER

*W*e cannot direct the wind, but we can adjust the sails.

DOLLY PARTON

*H*appiness comes from . . . some curious adjustment to life.

HUGH WALPOLE

Authenticity

*W*e need a deeper sense of who we are, and an acceptable balance between our social self and our essential self, following our North Star, to be fully present as conscious beings, before we can presume to lead others.

LANCE SECRETAN

*A*uthenticity is a collection of choices that we have to make every day. It's about the choice to show up and be real. The choice to be honest. The choice to let our true selves be seen.

BRENÉ BROWN

*T*he authentic self is the Soul made visible.

SARAH BAN BREATHNACH

*T*he most authentic thing about us is our capacity to create, to overcome, to endure, to transform, to love and to be greater than our suffering.

BEN OKRI

*B*e yourself; everyone else is taken.

OSCAR WILDE

*A*uthentic empowerment is the knowing that you are on purpose, doing God's work, peacefully and harmoniously.

DR. WAYNE W. DYER

*A*uthenticity empowers communication.

JAMES L. NICODEM

*T*oday you are You, that is truer than true. There is no one alive who is Youer than You.

DR. SEUSS

*H*ard times arouse an instinctive desire for authenticity.

COCO CHANEL

*B*e yourself. The world worships the original.

JEAN COCTEAU

*T*he level of success you achieve depends on your mindset, motivation and ability to live authentically as your true self.

SANDRA HANESWORTH

Beliefs/Mind-Set

*T*he thing always happens that you really believe in; and the belief in a thing makes it happen.

FRANK LLOYD WRIGHT

*S*top settling for less than you deserve, both personally and professionally; life is just too short.

KATRINA SAWA

You're only limited by the parameters of your own mind.

CHRISTOPHER RAUSCH

You are the carpenter of your mind—where you have built a wall, you also have the ability to build a door that can open your life to great riches.

VALERIE BRUNNBERG

Yes, I know that you feel you are not strong enough. That's what the enemy thinks too. But we're gonna fool them.

KNUTE ROCKNE

Never say can't.

JENNIFER BRICKER

Approach the game with no preset agendas and you'll probably come away surprised at your overall efforts.

PHIL JACKSON

Behind every kick of the ball there has to be a thought.

DENNIS BERGKAMP

Beliefs determine your results. Results reinforce your beliefs.

MARYANN EHMANN

Your time is limited, so don't waste it living some-one else's life. Don't be trapped by dogma—which is living with the results of other people's thinking. Don't let the noise of other's opinions drown out your own inner voice. And most important, have the courage to follow your heart and intuition. They somehow already know what you truly want to become. Everything else is secondary.

STEVE JOBS

Football is football and talent is talent. But the mindset of your team makes all the difference.

ROBERT GRIFFIN III

Clarity

Clarity breeds mastery.

ROBIN SHARMA

Gratitude unlocks the fullness of life. It turns what we have into enough, and more. It turns denial into acceptance, chaos to order, confusion to clarity. It can turn a meal into a feast, a house into a home, a stranger into a friend. Gratitude makes sense of our past, brings peace for today, and creates a vision for tomorrow.

MELODY BEATTIE

Clarity of mind means clarity of passion, too: this is why a great and clear mind loves ardently and sees distinctly what he loves.

BLAISE PASCAL

*I*t's a lack of clarity that creates chaos and frustration. Those emotions are poison to any living goal.

DR. STEVE MARABOLI

*P*eople are remarkably bad at remembering long lists of goals. I learned this at a professional level when trying to get my high-performance coaching clients to stay on track; the longer their lists of to-dos and goals, the more overwhelmed and off-track they got. Clarity comes with simplicity.

BRENDON BURCHARD

*C*larity affords focus.

THOMAS LEONARD

*C*larity is the most important thing. I can compare clarity to pruning in gardening. You know, you need to be clear. If you are not clear, nothing is going to happen. You have to be clear. Then you have to be confident about your vision. And after that, you just have to put a lot of work in.

DIANE VON FURSTENBERG

*Y*ou could write a song about some kind of emotional problem you are having, but it would not be a good song, in my eyes, until it went through a period of sensitivity to a moment of clarity. Without that moment of clarity to contribute to the song, it's just complaining.

JONI MITCHELL

*T*he great thing about a song is that no one has to know your story. But if you tell it in a way that has clarity and means something to somebody else, then it can apply to their story.

AMY GRANT

*I*t's weird that the greatest moments of clarity occur during moments of such confusion and stress.

NISHAN PANWAR

*F*or me the greatest beauty always lies in the greatest clarity.

GOTTHOLD EPHRAIM LESSING

Coachable

*T*he very best, those who experience long-term success, are those who are open to coaching.

DR. DEBORAH J. HRIVNAK

[*U*ncoachable players] do not help themselves or their teams by taking such a hard-headed approach to the game.

MARK MILLER

*I*n my experience, my most coachable clients have all shared at least these characteristics . . . humility (because they know there is always more to learn), high self-esteem (because they don't take constructive criticism as a personal attack), courage (because they willingly attempt even the most challenging or intimidating tasks), ambition (because they have a vision they want to achieve).

KELLIE COWLES

*O*nce the person commits to being coached, s/he begins to experience a different, more hopeful world as his or her perceptions evolve.

JOHN G. AGNO

*B*eing lead is not the same as giving up control.

LUKA FATUESI

*L*isten to what your coaches say, not to how they say it.

LINDSEY WILSON

*L*istening is such a simple act. It requires us to be present, and that takes practice, but we don't have to do anything else. We don't have to advise, or coach, or sound wise. We just have to be willing to sit there and listen.

MARGARET J. WHEATLEY

*D*ogs have boundless enthusiasm but no sense of shame. I should have a dog as a life coach.

MOBY

*N*o coach has ever won a game by what he knows; it's what his players know that counts.

PAUL BRYANT

*T*he best professionals at all levels (and in most fields) require coaching to improve and they know it. Are you one of them?

SAM PARKER

*T*o succeed in this, or at anything, you have to prepare yourself. That means you have to be open, be coachable, and willing to learn. If there is a training session, go to it. If there is a meeting, be there. Do whatever it takes.

TAMMI FUGGIT

Collaborate

*A*lone we can do so little; together we can do so much.

HELEN KELLER

*I*f everyone is moving forward together, then success takes care of itself.

HENRY FORD

*U*nity is strength . . . when there is teamwork and collaboration, wonderful things can be achieved.

MATTIE STEPANEK

*C*reating a better world requires teamwork, partnerships, and collaboration, as we need an entire army of companies to work together to build a better world within the next few decades. This means corporations must embrace the benefits of cooperating with one another.

SIMON MAINWARING

*W*hen I was a kid, there was no collaboration; it's you with a camera bossing your friends around. But as an adult, filmmaking is all about appreciating the talents of the people you surround yourself with and knowing you could never have made any of these films by yourself.

STEVEN SPIELBERG

*C*ollaboration is the best way to work. It's only way to work, really. Everyone's there because they have a set of skills to offer across the board.

ANTONY STARR

*A*s you navigate through the rest of your life, be open to collaboration. Other people and other people's ideas are often better than your own. Find a group of people who challenge and inspire you, spend a lot of time with them, and it will change your life.

AMY POEHLER

*L*ife is not a solo act. It's a huge collaboration, and we all need to assemble around us the people who care about us and support us in times of strife.

TIM GUNN

*T*he secret is to gang up on the problem, rather than each other.

THOMAS STALLKAMP

*O*pen collaboration encourages greater accountability, which in turn fosters trust.

RON GARAN

*W*e could learn a lot from crayons; some are sharp, some are pretty, some are dull, while others are bright, some have weird names, but we have to learn to live in the same box.

ROBERT FULGHUM

Commitment

*Q*uit making excuses. What we're really talking about here is commitment. Until you make a commitment to your dream, it's not a commitment at all. It's just another fantasy. And fantasies don't come true because they're not real, we're not committed to them. When we make commitments, they become dreams. And dreams are very real.

RUDY RUETTIGER

*I*t's not the will to win, but the will to prepare to win that makes the difference.

PAUL BRYANT

*T*oday I will do what others won't, so tomorrow I can accomplish what others can't.

JERRY RICE

*T*here are only two options regarding commitment. You're either in or you're out. There is no such thing as life in-between.

PAT RILEY

*C*ommit yourself to something you have a passion for.

BILL WALSH

*T*he quality of a person's life is in direct proportion to their commitment to excellence, regardless of their chosen field of endeavor.

VINCE LOMBARDI

*S*eems to me that there is a fine line between insanity and dedication . . . I call that line commitment.

JEREMY ALDANA

*T*here's a difference between interest and commitment. When you're interested in doing something, you do it only when circumstance permit. When you're committed to something, you accept no excuses, only results.

ART TUROCK

*Y*our mission isn't a project to check off your list. It's a commitment to which to dedicate your life.

VICTORIA MORAN

*T*here's no abiding success without commitment.

TONY ROBBINS

*L*osers make promises they often break. Winners make commitments they always keep.

DENIS WAITLEY

Communication

*L*istening is such a simple act. It requires us to be present, and that takes practice, but we don't have to do anything else. We don't have to advise, or coach, or sound wise. We just have to be willing to sit there and listen.

MARGARET J. WHEATLEY

*C*ommunication is a skill that you can learn. If you're willing to work at it, you can rapidly improve the quality of every part of your life.

BRIAN TRACY

*T*he most important thing in communication is hearing what isn't said.

PETER DRUCKER

*Y*our ability to communicate is an important tool in your pursuit of your goals, whether it is with your family, your co-workers or your clients and customers.

LES BROWN

A lot of problems in the world would disappear if we talk to each other instead of about each other.

UNKNOWN

*T*ake advantage of every opportunity to practice your communication skills so that when important occasions arise, you will have the fit, the style, the sharpness, the clarity, and the emotions to affect other people.

JIM ROHN

*G*ood communication is as stimulating as black coffee and just as hard to sleep after.

ANNE MORROW LINDBERGH

*T*he basic building block of good communications is the feeling that every human being is unique and of value.

UNKNOWN

*T*he single biggest problem in communication is the illusion that it has taken place.

GEORGE BERNARD SHAW

*C*ommunication is a skill that you can learn. It's like riding a bicycle or typing. If you're willing to work at it, you can rapidly improve the quality of every part of your life.

BRIAN TRACY

*T*he three fastest means of communication: telephone, television, and tell a woman.

UNKNOWN

Confidence

*T*he way to develop self-confidence is to do the thing you fear and get a record of successful experiences behind you.

WILLIAM JENNINGS BRYAN

*L*ow self-confidence isn't a life sentence. Self-confidence can be learned, practiced, and mastered—just like any other skill. Once you master it, everything in your life will change for the better.

BARRIE DAVENPORT

*C*onfidence doesn't come out of nowhere. It's a result of something . . . hours and days and weeks and years of constant work and dedication.

ROGER STAUBACH

*W*hen you have confidence, you can have a lot of fun. And when you have fun, you can do amazing things.

JOE NAMATH

*W*ho has self-confidence will lead the rest.

HORACE

*I*f you never struggle with confidence, you obviously are not stretching yourself far enough. You are not pressing to the edge of your abilities. In other words, the only way to never struggle with confidence is to play it safe. Play it known. Play it in a way that you achieve stability, but lose opportunity.

TIMOTHY URSINY

*T*otal self-confidence is built through positive expectations. You can build positive expectations by knowing that you have the power within to overcome any obstacle that lies ahead. So many people have a magnetic attraction to the past. They save mementos, clippings, old letters, and trivia. There is nothing wrong with this, but if you want to succeed, your mind must focus on where you are going, not on where you have been. Instead of saving mementos, clippings, old letters, and trivia from the past, it would be more productive to make a scrapbook with pictures of where you want to go and what you want to be in the future.

ROBERT ANTHONY

*N*ever forget, only dead fish swim with the stream.

MALCOLM MUGGERIDGE

*C*rystallize your goals. Make a plan for achieving them and set yourself a deadline. Then, with supreme confidence, determination and disregard for obstacles and other people's criticisms, carry out your plan.

PAUL MEYER

*C*onfidence is contagious. So is lack of confidence.

VINCE LOMBARDI

*A*nyone who ever gave you confidence, you owe them a lot.

TRUMAN CAPOTE

Courage

*Y*ou can learn more character on the two-yard line than anywhere else in life.

PAUL DIETZEL

*I*f you hear a voice within you say "you cannot paint," then by all means paint, and that voice will be silenced.

VINCENT VAN GOGH

*H*e who is not courageous enough to take risks will accomplish nothing in life.

MUHAMMAD ALI

*C*ourage is what it takes to stand up and speak; courage is also what it takes to sit down and listen.

WINSTON CHURCHILL

*H*ow few there are who have courage enough to own their faults, or resolution enough to mend them.

BENJAMIN FRANKLIN

*C*ourage is grace under pressure.

ERNEST HEMINGWAY

*O*nly those who will risk going too far can possibly find out how far one can go.

T. S. ELIOT

*Y*ou will never do anything in this world without courage. It is the greatest quality of the mind next to honor.

ARISTOTLE

*I*f you are lucky enough to find a way of life you love, you have to find the courage to live it.

JOHN IRVING

*C*ourage is fear holding on a minute longer.

GEORGE S. PATTON

*I*t is curious that physical courage should be so common in the world and moral courage so rare.

MARK TWAIN

Decision Making

*W*e need to accept that we won't always make the right decisions, that we'll screw up royally sometimes—understanding that failure is not the opposite of success, it's part of success.

ARIANNA HUFFINGTON

*H*aving a clear understanding of your values and your commitment to live by them makes decision making easier, especially when you're faced with conflicting desires.

NANCY MATTHEWS

*W*e make decisions out of love or fear. I choose love.

NICOLE RHOADES

*I*t is in your moments of decision that your destiny is shaped.

TONY ROBBINS

*T*here was no time to think, I just hit it.

ANDRES INIESTA

*W*hen you have to make a choice and don't make it, that is in itself a choice.

WILLIAM JAMES

*I*t's not hard to make decisions when you know what your values are.

ROY E. DISNEY

*S*ome persons are very decisive when it comes to avoiding decisions.

BRENDAN FRANCIS

*G*ood decisions come from experience, and experience comes from bad decisions.

MARK TWAIN

*O*nce you make a decision, the universe conspires to make it happen.

RALPH WALDO EMERSON

*I*nability to make decisions is one of the principal reasons executives fail. Deficiency in decision-making ranks much higher than lack of specific knowledge or technical know-how as an indicator of leadership failure.

JOHN C. MAXWELL

Determination

*T*he power is in the work. You do the work, you will have the power.

ELDONNA LEWIS FERNANDEZ

*I*n life, as in a football game, the principle to follow is: Hit the line hard.

THEODORE ROOSEVELT

*H*ave you ever noticed, that the things in life for which you are most proud, are also the things in life, for which you have worked the hardest?

JOHN A. HRIVNAK

*W*e must look for ways to be an active force in our own lives. We must take charge of our own destinies, design a life of substance and truly begin to live our dreams.

LES BROWN

*T*he difference between the impossible and the possible lies in a person's determination.

TOMMY LASORDA

*W*inners are ordinary people with extraordinary determination.

UNKNOWN

What does it take to be a champion? Desire, dedication, determination, concentration and the will to win.

PATTY BERG

If I had to select one quality, one personal characteristic that I regard as being most highly correlated with success, whatever the field, I would pick the trait of persistence. Determination. The will to endure to the end, to get knocked down seventy times and get up off the floor saying, "Here comes number seventy-one!"

RICHARD DEVOS

I am not discouraged, because every wrong attempt discarded is another step forward.

THOMAS EDISON

Gold medals aren't really made of gold. They're made of sweat, determination, and a hard-to-find alloy called guts.

DAN GABLE

A determined person will do more with a pen and paper, than a lazy person will accomplish with a personal computer.

CATHERINE PULSIFER

Discipline

I don't want to win enough to be placed on NCAA probation, I just want to win enough to warrant an investigation.

BOB DEVANEY

*D*iscipline yourself and others won't need to.

JOHN WOODEN

*T*o me, discipline in football occurs on the field, not off it.

JOHN MADDEN

*R*ule your mind or it will rule you.

HORACE

*T*he only discipline that lasts is self-discipline.

BUM PHILLIPS

*T*he first and best victory is to conquer self.

PLATO

*T*alent without discipline is like an octopus on roller skates. There's plenty of movement, but you never know if it's going to be forward, backwards, or sideways.

H. JACKSON BROWN JR.

*I*f we don't discipline ourselves, the world will do it for us.

WILLIAM FEATHER

*S*uccess is nothing more than a few simple disciplines, practiced every day.

JIM ROHN

*T*he individual who wants to reach the top in business must appreciate the might and force of habit. He must be quick to break those habits that can break him—and hasten to adopt those practices that will become the habits that help him achieve the success he desires.

J. PAUL GETTY

*W*hat we do upon some great occasion will probably depend on what we already are. What we are will be the result of previous years of self-discipline.

HENRY LIDDON

Dreams

*I*f one advances confidently in the direction of his dreams, and endeavors to live the life which he has imagined, he will meet with a success unexpected in common hours.

HENRY DAVID THOREAU

*D*reams are lovely. But they are just dreams. Fleeting, ephemeral, pretty. But dreams do not come true just because you dream them. It's hard work that makes things happen. It's hard work that creates change.

SHONDA RHIMES

*T*ell others your dreams and they'll help them come true.

DAVE BASTIEN

*A*ll our dreams can come true, if we have the courage to pursue them.

WALT DISNEY

*W*hen you cease to dream you cease to live.

MALCOLM FORBES

*C*ommitment leads to action. Action brings your dream closer.

MARCIA WIEDER

*H*elp others achieve their dreams and you will achieve yours.

LES BROWN

*D*on't ever let someone whose given up on their dreams, talk you out of pursuing yours.

UNKNOWN

*I*f you keep chasing after your dreams, and do not seize to ascertain them, in time you will catch that dream you so desire.

ANDREW GUZALDO

*N*o one has ever achieved anything from the smallest to the greatest unless the dream was dreamed first.

LAURA INGALLS WILDER

*D*reams are the seedlings of reality.

JAMES ALLEN

Enthusiasm

*E*nthusiasm moves the world.

ARTHUR BALFOUR

*H*ow do you go from where you are to where you wanna be? And I think you have to have an enthusiasm for life. You have to have a dream, a goal. And you have to be willing to work for it.

JIM VALVANO

*E*nthusiasm is the yeast that makes your hopes shine to the stars. Enthusiasm is the sparkle in your eyes, the swing in your gait. The grip of your hand, the irresistible surge of will and energy to execute your ideas.

HENRY FORD

*T*oday is life-the only life you are sure of. Make the most of today. Get interested in something. Shake yourself awake. Develop a hobby. Let the winds of enthusiasm sweep through you. Live today with gusto.

DALE CARNEGIE

*T*here is a real magic in enthusiasm. It spells the difference between mediocrity and accomplishment.

NORMAN VINCENT PEALE

*W*hen you discover your mission, you will feel its demand. It will fill you with enthusiasm and a burning desire to get to work on it.

W. CLEMENT STONE

A man can succeed at almost anything for which he has unlimited enthusiasm.

CHARLES M. SCHWAB

*G*et excited and enthusiastic about you own dream. This excitement is like a forest fire—you can smell it, taste it, and see it from a mile away.

DENIS WAITLEY

*I*f you aren't fired with enthusiasm, you will be fired with enthusiasm.

VINCE LOMBARDI

$\mathcal{B}$e enthusiastic as a leader. You can't light a fire with a wet match!

UNKNOWN

$\mathcal{E}$nthusiasm makes ordinary people extraordinary.

UNKNOWN

Focus

$\mathcal{S}$on, you've got a good engine, but your hands aren't on the steering wheel.

BOBBY BOWDEN

$\mathcal{O}$ne reason so few of us achieve what we truly want is that we never direct our focus; we never concentrate our power. Most people dabble their way through life, never deciding to master anything in particular.

TONY ROBBINS

$\mathcal{T}$o inspire a singularity of focus, a challenge must be important to you and it must be something you feel you should do now in this moment. If it's trivial or not time-bound, you won't engage. So in selecting your next challenge in life, choose one that is meaningful and will demand your complete concentration.

BRENDON BURCHARD

*T*he key to success is to focus our conscious mind on things we desire not things we fear.

BRIAN TRACY

*T*he successful man is the average man, focused.

UNKNOWN

*F*ocus on the journey, not the destination. Joy is found not in finishing activity but in doing it.

GREG ANDERSON

*M*ost people have no idea of the giant capacity we can immediately command when we focus all of our resources on mastering a single area of our lives.

TONY ROBBINS

A person who aims at nothing is sure to hit it.

UNKNOWN

*W*hat do I mean by concentration? I mean focusing totally on the business at hand and commanding your body to do exactly what you want it to do.

ARNOLD PALMER

*F*ocusing isn't just an optical activity, it is also a mental one.

BRIDGET RILEY

*Y*ou don't get results by focusing on results. You get results by focusing on the actions that produce results.

MIKE HAWKINS

Goals

*P*eople with clear, written goals, accomplish far more in a shorter period of time than people without them could ever imagine.

BRIAN TRACY

*T*hat's why at the start of every season I always encouraged players to focus on the journey rather than the goal. What matters most is, playing the game the right way and having the courage to grow, as human beings as well as basketball players. When you do that, the ring takes care of itself.

PHIL JACKSON

*T*he trouble with not having a goal is that you can spend your life running up and down the field and never score.

BILL COPELAND

A goal is a dream with a deadline.

NAPOLEON HILL

Setting a goal is not the main thing. It is deciding how you will go about achieving it and staying with that plan.

TOM LANDRY

You are never too old to set another goal or to dream a new dream.

C. S. LEWIS

Goals. There's no telling what you can do when you get inspired by them. There's no telling what you can do when you believe in them. There's no telling what will happen when you act upon them.

JIM ROHN

People with goals succeed because they know where they are going . . . It's as simple as that.

EARL NIGHTINGALE

We aim above the mark to hit the mark.

RALPH WALDO EMERSON

Set your goals high enough to inspire you and low enough to encourage you.

UNKNOWN

Begin with the end in mind.

STEPHEN COVEY

Health

*I*nner happiness and joy are the fuel to magnificent health.

KRISTEN SHARMA

*L*ife becomes extraordinary when we discover that being absolutely committed to taking care of ourselves, leads to abundance in every aspect of our lives.

SUSAN SHEPHERD

*T*he data suggest that to have a thriving day, we need six hours of social time.

TOM RATH

*A*ll you need is love. But a little chocolate now and then doesn't hurt.

CHARLES M. SCHULZ

*Y*ou only live once, but if you do it right, once is enough.

MAE WEST

*D*on't suffer from insanity. Enjoy every minute of it.

UNKNOWN

*T*he greatest wealth is health.

VIRGIL

*L*ife expectancy would grow by leaps and bounds if green vegetables smelled as good as bacon.

DOUG LARSON

*I*n order to change we must be sick and tired of being sick and tired.

UNKNOWN

*I*f I'd known I was going to live so long, I'd have taken better care of myself.

LEON ELDRED

*I*t's more than what you eat or how often you exercise. It's even more than just essential steps to wellness. It's energy to fully live the game of life.

TONY ROBBINS

Inspiration

*I*f you feel the urge to do something good, just do it!

DR. SUNIL SHARMA

*Y*ou can learn a line from a win and a book from a defeat.

PAUL BROWN

*G*ood players inspire themselves. Great players inspire others.

UNKNOWN

*B*egin doing what you want to do now. We are not living in eternity. We have only this moment, sparkling like a star in our hand—and melting like a snowflake.

MARIE BEYON RAY

*N*othing splendid has ever been achieved except by those who dared believe that something inside them was superior to circumstance.

BRUCE BARTON

*T*wo roads diverged in a wood, and I— / I took the one less traveled by, / And that has made all the difference.

ROBERT FROST

*P*eople often say that motivation doesn't last. Well, neither does bathing. That's why we recommend it daily.

ZIG ZIGLAR

*I*t's not the years in your life that count. It's the life in your years.

ABRAHAM LINCOLN

*O*ur lives begin to end the day we become silent about things that matter.

MARTIN LUTHER KING JR.

We may not always get what we want, but we always become what we want.

DAVID TIMMS

If you want to achieve greatness, stop asking for permission.

UNKNOWN

Kindness

Treat people as if they were what they ought to be and you help them to become what they are capable of being.

JOHANN WOLFGANG VON GOETHE

Your greatness is measured by your kindness; your education and intellect by your modesty; your ignorance is betrayed by your suspicions and prejudices, and your real caliber is measured by the consideration and tolerance you have for others.

WILLIAM J. H. BOETCKER

When I was young I admired clever people. Now that I am old, I admire kind people.

ABRAHAM JOSHUA HESCHEL

What wisdom can you find that is greater than kindness?

JEAN-JACQUES ROUSSEAU

*W*herever there is a human being, there is an opportunity for kindness.

SENECA

*T*oo often we underestimate the power of a touch, a smile, a kind word, a listening ear, an honest compliment, or the smallest act of caring all of which have the potential to turn a life around.

LEO BUSCAGLIA

*W*e can let the circumstances of our lives harden us so that we become increasingly resentful and afraid, or we can let them soften us, and make us kinder. We always have the choice.

DALAI LAMA

*T*here are those who are in need of some loving kindness in the unique way that you can provide.

LYNNE NAMKA

*T*he smallest act of kindness is worth more than the grandest intention.

OSCAR WILDE

*T*he seeds of kindness that you plant today, will one day bloom in the hearts of all that you touch.

UNKNOWN

*L*abels are for soup cans . . . not for people.

SANDRA HANESWORTH

Momentum

Either you run the day, or the day runs you.

JIM ROHN

Start where you are. Use what you have. Do what you can.

ARTHUR ASHE

People who succeed have momentum. The more they succeed, the more they want to succeed, and the more they find a way to succeed. Similarly, when someone is failing, the tendency is to get on a downward spiral that can even become a self-fulfilling prophecy.

TONY ROBBINS

We got that momentum going, got in a rhythm, and you saw (that) once we get into it, we can do pretty much anything we want to . . . We've got to get into that rhythm every game.

BRIAN BROHM

Most of life is routine—dull and grubby, but routine is the momentum that keeps a man going. If you wait for inspiration you'll be standing on the corner after the parade is a mile down the street.

BEN NICHOLAS

*M*omentum? Momentum is the next day's starting pitcher.

EARL WEAVER

*S*ometimes thinking too much can destroy your
momentum.

TOM WATSON

*F*or any movement to gain momentum, it must
start with a small action. This action becomes
multiplied by the masses, and is made tangible when
leadership changes course due to the weight of the
movement's voice.

ADAM BRAUN

*T*he BIG push means being able to develop and sustain momentum toward your goal; it is the process of actively replacing excuses with winning habits,
the ultimate excuses blockers. Moreover, it is being
willing to go to the wall for what you want or believe
in, to push beyond your previous mental and physical
limits, no matter what it takes.

LORII MYERS

*U*nwavering incremental change can create
remarkable and monumental results.

RYAN LILLY

*W*hat lies behind us and what lies ahead of us are tiny matters compared to what lives within us.

HENRY STANLEY HASKINS

Opportunity

*L*ife opens up opportunities to you, and you either take them or you stay afraid of taking them.

JIM CARREY

*A*t this very moment, exactly where you are, you are surrounded by boundless opportunity! It does not matter your circumstance, your past mistakes, what you have or have not done. You are living in a field of infinite awareness, unlimited possibilities. All that remains is for you to awaken to the potential that surrounds you, to open your eyes that you might see.

ROBERT SIDELL

*L*uck is what happens at the intersection of preparation and opportunity.

SENECA

I feel that luck is preparation meeting opportunity.

OPRAH WINFREY

*I*f opportunity doesn't knock, build a door.

MILTON BERLE

*A*sk and it will be given to you; search, and you will find; knock and the door will be opened for you.

JESUS

*W*hen one door of happiness closes, another opens, but often we look so long at the closed door that we do not see the one that has been opened for us.

HELEN KELLER

*I*f you're offered a seat on a rocket ship, don't ask what seat! Just get on.

SHERYL SANDBERG

*O*pportunities don't happen, you create them.

CHRIS GROSSER

*T*ake a lesson from the mosquito. She never waits for an opening—she makes one.

KIRK KIRKPATRICK

*T*he pessimist sees difficulty in every opportunity. The optimist sees the opportunity in every difficulty.

WINSTON CHURCHILL

Optimism

*A*n optimist is someone who goes after Moby Dick in a rowboat and takes the tartar sauce with him.

ZIG ZIGLAR

*S*ome folks go through life pleased that the glass is half full. Others spend a lifetime lamenting that it's half-empty. The truth is: There is a glass with a certain volume of liquid in it. From there, it's up to you!

DR. JAMES S. VUOCOLO

*N*o pessimist ever discovered the secrets of the stars, or sailed to an uncharted land, or opened a new heaven to the human spirit.

HELEN KELLER

*A*lways look on the bright side of life. Otherwise, it'll be too dark to read.

UNKNOWN

*T*he average pencil is seven inches long, with just a half-inch eraser-in case you thought optimism was dead.

ROBERT BRAULT

*B*oth optimists and pessimists contribute to our society. The optimist invents the airplane and the pessimist the parachute.

GIL STERN

Of course, I look at the glass half full. The only time I would look at it half empty is when I think about how good the first half tasted.

DREW DEYOUNG

There is no sadder sight than a young pessimist.

MARK TWAIN

Aerodynamically, the bumble bee shouldn't be able to fly, but the bumble bee doesn't know it so it goes on flying anyway.

MARY KAY ASH

Believe you can and you're halfway there.

THEODORE ROOSEVELT

Optimism is a happiness magnet. If you stay positive, good things and good people will be drawn to you.

MARY LOU RETTON

Passion

Purpose is the reason you journey. Passion is the fire that lights your way.

UNKNOWN

*H*ow wonderful it is that nobody need wait a single moment before starting to improve the world.

ANNE FRANK

*D*on't be normal. Sadly, normal is getting dressed in clothes that you buy for work and driving through traffic in a car that you financed, in order to get to the job that you don't really like, but that you need, to pay for the clothes and the car, and the house you leave vacant all day so you can afford to live in it.

UNKNOWN

I would rather die of passion than of boredom.

VINCENT VAN GOGH

*T*here is no greatness without a passion to be great, whether it's the aspiration of an athlete or an artist, a scientist, a parent, or a businessperson.

TONY ROBBINS

*O*ne person with passion is better than forty people merely interested.

E. M. FORSTER

*C*hase your passion, not your pension.

DENIS WAITLEY

*W*hen passion and skill work together, the end result is often a masterpiece.

CHRIS GUILLEBEAU

*N*othing great in the world has ever been accomplished without passion.

Georg Wilhelm Friedrich Hegel

*P*assion will move men beyond themselves, beyond their shortcomings, beyond their failures.

Joseph Campbell

*P*assion is the genesis of genius.

Galileo Galilei

Perseverance/Persistence

*I*f people knew how hard I worked to get my mastery, it wouldn't seem so wonderful after all.

Michelangelo

I'm convinced that about half of what separates the successful entrepreneur from the non-successful entrepreneur is pure perseverance.

Steve Jobs

*T*he question isn't who is going to let me; it's who is going to stop me.

Ayn Rand

A real entrepreneur is somebody who has no safety net underneath them.

Henry Kravis

*N*o person was ever honored for what he received. Honor has been the reward for what he gave.

CALVIN COOLIDGE

*Y*ou cannot create life experience-you must undergo it.

ALBERT CAMUS

*T*wenty years from now you will be more disappointed by the things that you didn't do than by the ones you did do, so throw off the bowlines, sail away from safe harbor, catch the trade winds in your sails. Explore, Dream, Discover.

MARK TWAIN

*E*very child is an artist. The problem is how to remain an artist once he grows up.

PABLO PICASSO

I didn't fail the test. I just found 100 ways to do it wrong.

BENJAMIN FRANKLIN

*T*here are no traffic jams along the extra mile.

ROGER STAUBACH

*N*o is a word on your path to Yes. Don't give up too soon. Not even if well-meaning parents, relatives, friends, and colleagues tell you to get a real job. Your dreams are your real job.

JOYCE SPIZER

Preparation

I don't celebrate because I'm only doing my job. When a postman delivers letters, does he celebrate?

MARIO BALOTELLI

*I*t's not the will to win that matters—everyone has that. It's the will to prepare to win that matters.

PAUL BRYANT

*T*he will to win is worthless if you do not have the will to prepare.

THANE YOST

*A*ll things are ready, if our minds be so.

WILLIAM SHAKESPEARE

*I*f I had eight hours to chop down a tree, I'd spend six sharpening my axe.

UNKNOWN

*I*f I miss a day of practice, I know it. If I miss two days, my manager knows it. If I miss three days, my audience knows it.

ANDRÉ PREVIN

*Y*ou cannot move forward in any project, or task, career, relationship or changing a habit unless you plan. And, preparation is not the end but only the beginning.

BYRON PULSIFER

*B*y failing to prepare you are preparing to fail.

BENJAMIN FRANKLIN

*E*xpect the best. Prepare for the worst. Capitalize on what comes.

ZIG ZIGLAR

*Y*ou don't run twenty-six miles at five minutes a mile on good looks and a secret recipe.

FRANK SHORTER

*S*pectacular achievement is always preceded by spectacular preparation.

ROBERT H. SCHULLER

Purpose

*I*f you don't know where you're going, any road will get you there.

LEWIS CARROLL

*M*aking money is not bad as long as you're doing something bigger than yourself. Live a life of purpose.

JEFF HOFFMAN

*I*t's not an accident that musicians become musicians and engineers become engineers: it's what they're born to do. If you can tune into your purpose and really align with it, setting goals so that your vision is an expression of that purpose, then life flows much more easily.

JACK CANFIELD

*T*he two most important days in your life are the day you are born and the day you find out why.

MARK TWAIN

*D*efiniteness of purpose is the starting point of all achievement.

W. CLEMENT STONE

*T*he meaning of life is to find your gift. The purpose of life is to give it away.

PABLO PICASSO

*M*y life has no purpose, no direction, no aim, no meaning, and yet I'm happy. I can't figure it out. What am I doing right?

CHARLES M. SCHULZ

*L*et others lead small lives, but not you. Let others argue over small things, but not you. Let others cry over small hurts, but not you. Let others leave their future in someone else's hands, but not you.

JIM ROHN

I'm not afraid; I was born to do this.

JOAN OF ARC

*T*he purpose of life is a life of purpose.

ROBERT BYRNE

*G*reat minds have purposes, others have wishes.

WASHINGTON IRVING

Resilience

*Y*ou've got to get over games and have the resiliency to come back.

JOHN GRUDEN

*I*f you're going through hell, keep going.

WINSTON CHURCHILL

*M*an never made any material as resilient as the human spirit.

BERNARD WILLIAMS

*P*eople who soar are those who refuse to sit back, sigh and wish things would change. They neither complain of their lot nor passively dream of some distant ship coming in. Rather, they visualize in their minds that they are not quitters; they will not allow life's circumstances to push them down and hold them under.

CHARLES R. SWINDOLL

*A*dversity has the effect of eliciting talents, which in prosperous circumstances would have lain dormant.

HORACE

*W*e could never learn to be brave and patient, if there were only joy in the world.

HELEN KELLER

*T*here are two ways of spreading light: to be the candle or the mirror that reflects it.

EDITH WHARTON

*L*ife doesn't get easier or more forgiving, we get stronger and more resilient.

DR. STEVE MARABOLI

*T*ough times don't last, tough people do.

ROBERT H. SCHULLER

I am not what happened to me, I am what I choose to become.

CARL JUNG

*T*he strongest oak of the forest is not the one that is protected from the storm and hidden from the sun. It's the one that stands in the open where it is compelled to struggle for its existence against the winds and rains and the scorching sun.

NAPOLEON HILL

Responsibility

*S*uccess on any major scale requires you to accept responsibility . . . In the final analysis, the only quality that all successful people have . . . is the ability to take on responsibility.

MICHAEL KORDA

*A*ccepting full responsibility for your life and your attitude is the first step in changing your situation.

JERRY LEVINSON

*Y*ou must take personal responsibility. You cannot change the circumstances, the seasons, or the wind, but you can change yourself.

Jim Rohn

*M*en who reject the responsibility of thought and reason can only exist as parasites on the thinking of others.

Ayn Rand

*I*n dreams begins responsibility.

W. B. Yeats

*T*he willingness to accept responsibility for one's own life is the source from which self-respect spring.

Joan Didion

*P*eak performance begins with your taking complete responsibility for your life and everything that happens to you.

Brian Tracy

*Y*ou cannot escape the responsibility of tomorrow by evading it today.

Abraham Lincoln

*A*ction springs not from thought, but from a readiness for responsibility.

DIETRICH BONHOEFFER

*T*hose who enjoy responsibility usually get it; those who merely like exercising authority usually lose it.

MALCOLM FORBES

*N*o individual raindrop ever considers itself responsible for the flood.

UNKNOWN

Skills

*T*here is no doubt at all in my mind that the old-time ballplayer was smarter than the modern ballplayer. Now the game is all power, lively balls, and shorter fences.

"WAHOO" SAM CRAWFORD

*Y*ou cannot be anything you want to be—but you can be a whole lot more of who you already are.

TOM RATH

*W*hen we're able to put most of our energy into developing our natural talents, extraordinary room for growth exists.

TOM RATH

I'm going to go out and be the best quarterback I can be and get the most out of my potential.

ELI MANNING

*E*nduring setbacks while maintaining the ability to show others the way to go forward is a true test of leadership.

NITIN NOHRIA

*W*hen I stand before God at the end of my life, I would hope that I would not have a single bit of talent left and could say, I used everything you gave me.

ERMA BOMBECK

*W*e must believe that we are gifted for something, and that this thing, at whatever cost, must be attained.

MARIE CURIE

*Y*ou can't use up creativity. The more you use, the more you have.

MAYA ANGELOU

*S*uccess requires first expending ten units of effort to produce one unit of results. Your momentum will then produce ten units of results with each unit of effort.

CHARLES J. GIVENS

The most important thing you can do to achieve your goals is to make sure that as soon as you set them, you immediately begin to create momentum.

TONY ROBBINS

The world is wide, and I will not waste my life in friction when it could be turned into momentum.

FRANCES WILLARD

Spiritual Practice

Meditation is a lifelong process. Give it a try. As you get deeper and more disciplined into the process, you'll get deeper and more disciplined in your mind and life.

BRENDON BURCHARD

Trust your heart and follow its whisper.

GLENN MORSHOWER

If you look at the world, you'll be distressed. If you look within, you'll be depressed. If you look at God you'll be at rest.

CORRIE TEN BOOM

When your life is filled with the desire to see the holiness in everyday life, something magical happens: ordinary life becomes extraordinary, and the very process of life begins to nourish your soul!

RABBI HAROLD KUSHNER

*L*earn to get in touch with the silence within yourself and know that everything in this life has a
purpose. There are no mistakes, no coincidences. All
events are blessings given to us to learn from.

ELIZABETH KÜBLER-ROSS

*W*e need silence to be alone with God, to speak to
him, to listen to him, to ponder his words deep
in our hearts. We need to be alone with God in silence
to be renewed and transformed. Silence gives us a new
outlook on life. In it we are filled with the energy of
God himself that makes us do all things with joy.

MOTHER TERESA

*P*rayer at its highest is a two-way conversation—
and for me the most important part is listening
to God's replies.

FRANK C. LAUBACH

*L*ook deep into nature, and then you will understand everything better.

ALBERT EINSTEIN

*O*pen your eyes and the whole world is full of God.

JAKOB BÖHME

*E*ach of us needs to withdraw from the cares which will not withdraw from us. We need hours of aimless wandering or spates of time sitting on park benches, observing the mysterious world of ants and the canopy of treetops.

MAYA ANGELOU

*P*rayer lays hold of God's plan and becomes the link between His will and its accomplishment on earth. Amazing things happen, and we are given the privilege of being the channels of the Holy Spirit's prayer.

ELISABETH ELLIOT

Values

*W*hen your values are clear to you, making decisions becomes easier.

ROY E. DISNEY

I started my life with a single absolute: that the world was mine to shape in the image of my highest values and never to be given up to a lesser standard, no matter how long or hard the struggle.

AYN RAND

*I*f you hang out with chickens, you're going to cluck and if you hang out with eagles, you're going to fly.

DR. STEVE MARABOLI

*I*f you don't set a baseline standard for what you'll accept in life, you'll find it's easy to slip into behaviors and attitudes or a quality of life that's far below what you deserve.

T<small>ONY</small> R<small>OBBINS</small>

*J*ust as your car runs more smoothly and requires less energy to go faster and farther when the wheels are in perfect alignment, you perform better when your thoughts, feelings, emotions, goals, and values are in balance.

B<small>RIAN</small> T<small>RACY</small>

A mission statement is not something you write overnight . . . But fundamentally, your mission statement becomes your constitution, the solid expression of your vision and values. It becomes the criterion by which you measure everything else in your life.

S<small>TEPHEN</small> C<small>OVEY</small>

*V*alues provide perspective in the best of times and the worst.

C<small>HARLES</small> G<small>ARFIELD</small>

*D*on't let your special character and values, the secret that you know and no one else does, the truth—don't let that get swallowed up by the great chewing complacency.

A<small>ESOP</small>

*T*hose who stand for nothing, fall for anything.

ALEXANDER HAMILTON

*I*t's easy to find people who understand costs. The challenge is to find people who understand values.

MICHAEL JOSEPHSON

*L*ive one day at a time emphasizing ethics rather than rules.

DR. WAYNE W. DYER

Vision

*V*ision, if it is anything, is your life story in action.

GREGG LEVOY

*G*reat vision without great people is irrelevant.

JAMES C. COLLINS

*I*n life, as in football, you won't go far unless you know where the goalposts are.

ARNOLD H. GLASGOW

*C*reate your magnificent life.

MARYANN EHMANN

*W*hatever you can do or dream you can, begin it. Boldness has genius, and magic and power in it. Begin it now.

WILLIAM HUTCHINSON MURRAY

*T*he greatest danger for most of us is not that our aim is too high and we miss it, but that it is too low and we reach it.

MICHELANGELO

*V*ision animates, inspires, transforms purpose into action.

WARREN BENNIS

*T*he future belongs to those who see possibilities before they become obvious.

JOHN SCULLY

*Y*ou cannot depend on your eyes when your imagination is out of focus.

MARK TWAIN

*I*f you limit your choices only to what seems possible or reasonable, you disconnect yourself from what you truly want, and all that is left is a compromise.

ROBERT FRITZ

*T*o the person who does not know where he wants to go there is no favorable wind.

SENECA

Vulnerable

*H*onesty and transparency make you vulnerable.
Be honest and transparent anyway.

MOTHER TERESA

*D*on't keep your heart safe . . . be vulnerable.

JOHN MAYER

*T*here can be no vulnerability without risk; there
can be no community without vulnerability;
there can be no peace, and ultimately no life, without
community.

M. SCOTT PECK

*O*wning our story can be hard but not nearly as
difficult as spending our lives running from it.
Embracing our vulnerabilities is risky but not nearly
as dangerous as giving up on love and belonging
and joy—the experiences that make us the most vulnerable. Only when we are brave enough to explore
the darkness will we discover the infinite power of
our light.

BRENÉ BROWN

I do not believe that sheer suffering teaches. If suffering alone taught, all the world would be wise, since
everyone suffers. To suffering must be added mourn-
ing, understanding, patience, love, openness and the
willingness to remain vulnerable.

ANNE MORROW LINDBERGH

When we were children, we used to think that when we were grown-up we would no longer be vulnerable. But to grow up is to accept vulnerability . . . To be alive is to be vulnerable.

MADELEINE L'ENGLE

If you truly pour your heart into what you believe in—even if it makes you vulnerable—amazing things can and will happen.

EMMA WATSON

Vulnerability is . . . about having the courage to show up and be seen.

BRENÉ BROWN

Be vulnerable. Allow yourself to feel, to be open and authentic. Tear down any emotional brick walls you have built around you and feel every exquisite emotion, both good and bad. This is real life. This is how you welcome new opportunities.

UNKNOWN

To love is to be vulnerable.

C. S. LEWIS

The fear of being vulnerable prompts me into bringing myself forward.

DAVID IGNATOW

PART IV

Postgame

---~/w~---

Acknowledge

*N*o one who achieves success does so without acknowledging the help of others. The wise and confident acknowledge this help with gratitude.

ALFRED NORTH WHITEHEAD

*D*esire for approval and recognition is a healthy motive, but the desire to be acknowledged as better, stronger, or more intelligent than a fellow being or fellow scholar easily leads to an excessively egoistic psychological adjustment, which may become injurious for the individual and for the community.

ALBERT EINSTEIN

*B*y appreciation, we make excellence in others our own property.

VOLTAIRE

*I*f human beings are perceived as potentials rather than problems, as possessing strengths instead of weaknesses, as unlimited rather that dull and unresponsive, then they thrive and grow to their capabilities.

BARBARA BUSH

*K*nowledge is in the end based on acknowledgement.

LUDWIG WITTGENSTEIN

*O*ne of the sanest, surest, and most generous joys of life comes from being happy over the good fortune of others.

ROBERT A. HEINLEIN

*T*he greatest need of every human being is the need for appreciation.

UNKNOWN

*W*hen I'm not thanked at all, I'm thanked enough, I've done my duty, and I've done no more.

HENRY FIELDING

*W*e are so often caught up in our destination that we forget to appreciate the journey, especially the goodness of the people we meet on the way. Appreciation is a wonderful feeling, don't overlook it.

UNKNOWN

*A*ppreciation of life itself, becoming suddenly aware of the miracle of being alive, on this planet, can turn what we call ordinary life into a miracle. We come awake to such a realization when we recognize our connection to a spiritual dimension.

Dan Wakefield

*I*n working with top leaders and thought philosophers of our time, I will tell you that among their secrets of success is a regular practice of acknowledging and appreciating what they have. It can offer an oracle into the future because it not only tells you where you are, but it also helps clarify where you want to go in life.

Jack Canfield

Contribution

*I*t's not about us. It's about showing up as our authentic selves and contributing to the lives of others.

Dr. Deborah J. Hrivnak

*W*hat we need to do is learn to work in the system, by which I mean that everybody, every team, every platform, every division, every component is there not for competitive profit or recognition, but for contribution to the system as a whole on a win-win basis.

W. Edwards Deming

The effect you have on others is the most valuable currency there is.

JIM CARREY

Try not to become a person of success, but rather try to become a person of value.

ALBERT EINSTEIN

Coming together is a beginning. Keeping together is progress. Working together is success.

HENRY FORD

The best executive is the one who has sense enough to pick good men to do what he wants done, and self-restraint enough to keep from meddling with them while they do it.

THEODORE ROOSEVELT

There is no such thing as a self-made man. You will reach your goals only with the help of others.

GEORGE SHINN

You're happiest when making the greatest contribution.

ROBERT KENNEDY

*R*elationship works best when you think of it as a vehicle of giving and contributing and as a secular spiritual practice, keeping your own interests present but not predominant in your choice processes.

PAUL RICHARDS

*H*ow lovely to think that no one need wait a moment, we can start now, start slowly changing the world! How lovely that everyone, great and small, can make their contribution toward introducing justice straightaway ... And you can always, always give something, even if it is only kindness!

ANNE FRANK

*W*hen you are making a success of something, it's not work. It's a way of life. You enjoy yourself because you are making your contribution to the world.

ANDY GRANATELLI

Faith

*L*eap and the net will appear.

JOHN BURROUGHS

*W*hy not take a chance on faith?

JIM CARREY

*F*aith is taking the first step even when you don't see the whole staircase.

MARTIN LUTHER KING JR.

*N*ever be afraid to trust an unknown future to a known God.

CORRIE TEN BOOM

*F*aith means living with uncertainty—feeling your way through life, letting your heart guide you like a lantern in the dark.

DAN MILLMAN

*F*aith is not about worry or care, but faith is fear that has said a prayer.

UNKNOWN

*F*rom time unknown to time unknown, / Eternal God, / Thou who madest heaven and earth, / give to us wisdom, prudence and strength, / give through Thy holy blessing faith unending.

HOWARD HANSON

*S*eek faith at all cost; it is the evidence of the answer of God.

REX ROUIS

*F*aith is believing that God is going to take you places before you even get there.

MATTHEW BARNETT

*F*aith means belief in something concerning which doubt is theoretically possible.

WILLIAM JAMES

I have learned that faith means trusting in advance what will only make sense in reverse.

PHILLIP YANCEY

Giving

*S*hare what you learn with others in your world to compound your interests.

BARRY DEMP

*W*e make a living by what we get. We make a life by what we give.

WINSTON CHURCHILL

*Y*our true worth is determined by how much more you give in value than you take in payment.

BOB BURG

*M*ost people just laugh when they hear that the secret to success is giving.

BOB BURG

You will get all you want in life, if you help enough other people get what they want.

ZIG ZIGLAR

Life isn't about getting and having, it's about giving and being.

KEVIN KRUSE

Successful entrepreneurs are givers and not takers of positive energy.

UNKNOWN

From what we get, we can make a living; what we give, however, makes a life.

ARTHUR ASHE

Happiness doesn't result from what we get, but from what we give.

BEN CARSON

Love only grows by sharing. You can only have more for yourself by giving it away to others.

BRIAN TRACY

Time is your most precious gift because you only have a set amount of it. You can make more money, but you can't make more time. When you give someone your time, you are giving them a portion of your life that you'll never get back. Your time is your life. That is why the greatest gift you can give someone is your time.

RICK WARREN

Gratitude

Gratitude unlocks the fullness of life. It turns what we have into enough, and more. It turns denial into acceptance, chaos to order, confusion to clarity. It can turn a mean into a feast, a house into a home, a stranger into a friend. Gratitude makes sense of our past, brings peace for today, and creates a vision for tomorrow.

MELODY BEATTIE

It is impossible to feel grateful and depressed in the same moment.

NAOMI WILLIAMS

Cultivate the habit of being grateful for every good thing that comes to you, and to give thanks continuously. And because all things have contributed to your advancement, you should include all things in your gratitude.

RALPH WALDO EMERSON

*P*iglet noticed that even though he had a Very Small Heart, it could hold a rather large amount of Gratitude.

A. A. MILNE

*I*n the end, though, maybe we must all give up trying to pay back the people in this world who sustain our lives. In the end, maybe it's wiser to surrender before the miraculous scope of human generosity and to just keep saying thank you, forever and sincerely, for as long as we have voices.

ELIZABETH GILBERT

*G*ratitude goes beyond the "mine" and "thine" and claims the truth that all of life is a pure gift. In the past I always thought of gratitude as a spontaneous response to the awareness of gifts received, but now I realize that gratitude can also be lived as a discipline. The discipline of gratitude is the explicit effort to acknowledge that all I am and have is given to me as a gift of love, a gift to be celebrated with joy.

HENRI J. M. NOUWEN

*G*ratitude is not only the greatest of virtues, but the parent of all others.

CICERO

*W*hen we give cheerfully and accept gratefully, everyone is blessed.

MAYA ANGELOU

*I*n life, one has a choice to take one of two paths: to wait for some special day—or to celebrate each special day.

RASHEED OGUNLARU

I truly believe we can either see the connections, celebrate them, and express gratitude for our blessings, or we can see life as a string of coincidences that have no meaning or connection. For me, I'm going to believe in miracles, celebrate life, rejoice in the views of eternity, and hope my choices will create a positive ripple effect in the lives of others. This is my choice.

MIKE ERICKSEN

*G*ratitude turns what we have into enough, and more. It turns denial into acceptance, chaos into order, confusion into clarity . . . it makes sense of our past, brings peace for today, and creates a vision for tomorrow.

MELODY BEATTIE

*D*evelop an attitude of gratitude, and give thanks for everything that happens to you, knowing that every step forward is a step toward achieving something bigger and better than your current situation.

BRIAN TRACY

Humility

A true leader is one who is humble enough to admit their mistakes.

UNKNOWN

I feel coming on a strange disease—humility.

FRANK LLOYD WRIGHT

*I*t is essential to employ, trust, and reward those whose perspective, ability, and judgment are radically different from yours. It is also rare, for it requires uncommon humility, tolerance, and wisdom.

DEE HOCK

*G*reat leaders don't need to act tough. Their confidence and humility serve to underscore their toughness.

SIMON SINEK

*L*ife is a long lesson in humility.

JAMES M. BARRIE

*H*umility is the true key to success. Successful people lose their way at times. They often embrace and overindulge from the fruits of success. Humility halts this arrogance and self-indulging trap. Humble people share the credit and wealth, remaining focused and hungry to continue the journey of success.

RICK PITINO

*T*rue humility is intelligent self respect which keeps us from thinking too highly or too meanly of ourselves. It makes us modest by reminding us how far we have come short of what we can be.

RALPH W. SOCKMAN

*E*arly in life I had to choose between honest arrogance and hypocritical humility. I chose the former and have seen no reason to change.

FRANK LLOYD WRIGHT

*B*lessed are the meek: for they shall inherit the earth.

MATTHEW 5:5

*H*umility is the only true wisdom by which we prepare our minds for all the possible changes of life.

GEORGE ARLISS

*O*n the highest throne in the world, we still sit only on our own bottom.

MICHEL DE MONTAIGNE

Integrity

*M*otivation without integrity is dangerous.

LARRY BROUGHTON

*I*ntegrity is choosing your thoughts and actions based on values rather than personal gain.

UNKNOWN

I never had a policy; I have just tried to do my very best each and every day.

ABRAHAM LINCOLN

*Y*ou do not wake up one morning a bad person. It happens by a thousand tiny surrenders of self-respect to self-interest.

ROBERT BRAULT

*L*ive so that when your children think of fairness, caring, and integrity, they think of you.

H. JACKSON BROWN JR.

*I*ntegrity is telling myself the truth. And honesty is telling the truth to other people.

SPENCER JOHNSON

*I*t takes less time to do a thing right than to explain why you did it wrong.

HENRY WADSWORTH LONGFELLOW

*Y*our reputation and integrity are everything. Follow through on what you say you're going to do. Your credibility can only be built over time, and it is built from the history of your words and actions.

MARIA RAZUMICH-ZEC

*W*aste no more time arguing about what a good man should be. Be one.

MARCUS AURELIUS

*I*ntegrity has no need of rules.

ALBERT CAMUS

A life lived with integrity—even if it lacks the trappings of fame and fortune is a shining star in whose light others may follow in the years to come.

DENIS WAITLEY

Legacy

*Y*our legacy is not going to be about championships and wins and losses. It's going to be about things that have to do with the development of players—spiritual matters—how players are treated, whether they grow personally or not.

RON BROWN

*T*ry not to become a man of success, but rather try to become a man of value.

ALBERT EINSTEIN

*Y*ou and I are players, God's our coach, and we're playing the biggest game of all. We have a loving God that made us. We need to get on His team.

JOE GIBBS

The most sought-after people in business today want more than just money and status. They want a greater sense of purpose and meaning in their work. They want to look in the mirror at the end of the day and know that they have made other people's lives better, that they have lived in alignment with their personal values and that they have fed their souls.

MURRAY THOMPSON

Seek for above all for a game worth playing.

ROBERT DE ROPP

Live life with no regrets, so you build a legacy instead of a lifestyle of mediocrity.

SANDRA HANESWORTH

If you play your heart out for what your jersey says on the front, everyone will remember what the jersey says on the back.

MIRACLE (US MEN'S HOCKEY TEAM FILM)

It's hard to beat a person who never gives up.

BABE RUTH

Heroes get remembered, but legends never die.

BABE RUTH

$\mathcal{T}$he game of life is a lot like football. You have to tackle your problems, block your fears, and score your points when you get the opportunity.

LEWIS GRIZZARD

$\mathcal{C}$arve your name on hearts, not tombstones. A legacy is etched into the minds of others and the stories they share about you.

SHANNON L. ALDER

$\mathcal{Y}$ou too can win Nobel Prizes. Study diligently. Respect DNA. Don't smoke. Don't drink. Avoid women and politics. That's my formula.

GEORGE BEADLE

Service

$\mathcal{W}$hen your dreams include service to others— accomplishing something that contributes to others—it also accelerates the accomplishment of that goal. People want to be part of something that contributes and makes a difference.

JACK CANFIELD

$\mathcal{W}$e are prone to judge success by the index of our salaries or the size of our automobiles rather than by the quality of our service and relationship to mankind.

MARTIN LUTHER KING JR.

Successful people are always looking for opportunities to help others. Unsuccessful people are always asking, "What's in it for me?"

BRIAN TRACY

Becoming one with the needs of others, instead of being separated from them, is the essence of service.

LANCE SECRETAN

When you get nervous, get into service.

DAVE VANHOOSE

In fact, in nearly every domain of our lives, if we have in our hearts the desire to serve others, we will be effective.

AL RITTER

Now the only way you can serve God on earth is by serving others.

RICK WARREN

The welfare of each is bound up in the welfare of all.

HELEN KELLER

If I have seen further it is by standing on the shoulders of giants.

ISAAC NEWTON

*I*t is literally true that you can succeed best and quickest by helping others to succeed.

NAPOLEON HILL

*H*appiness . . . consists in giving, and in serving others.

HENRY DRUMMOND

Team

*T*here is no such thing as a self-made millionaire, it takes a team.

LORAL LANGEMEIER

*I*t's not any one person. It's not any one coach. It's the team.

BRIAN MCBRIDE

*T*he secret is to work less as individuals and more as a team. As a coach, I play not my eleven best, but my best eleven.

KNUTE ROCKNE

*P*eople who work together will win, whether it be against complex football defenses, or the problems of modern society.

VINCE LOMBARDI

*I*f a team is to reach its potential, each player must be willing to subordinate his personal goals for the good of the team.

BUD WILKINSON

*T*he important thing to recognize is that it takes a team, and the team ought to get credit for the wins and the losses. Successes have many fathers, failures have none.

PHILIP CALDWELL

*I*ndividual commitment to a group effort—that is what makes a team work, a company work, a society work, a civilization work.

VINCE LOMBARDI

*I*t is easy to become a winner if you're simply willing to learn from those who have been winners. Find out who has had the most success at what they do. Watch their technique, observe their methods, and study their behavior. Listen and learn from the people who have achieved what you desire.

MIKE SHANAHAN

*T*he strength of the team is each individual member. The strength of each member is the team.

PHIL JACKSON

*T*he way a team plays as a whole determines its success. You may have the greatest bunch of individual stars in the world, but if they don't play together, the club won't be worth a dime.

BABE RUTH

*O*nly by binding together as a single force will we remain strong and unconquerable.

CHRIS BRADFORD

Truth

*W*e don't get to choose what is true. We only get to choose what we do about it.

KAMI GARCIA

*H*onesty is a very expensive gift—don't expect it from cheap people.

WARREN BUFFETT

*R*ather than love, than money, than fame, give me truth.

HENRY DAVID THOREAU

*I*f you tell the truth, you don't have to remember anything.

MARK TWAIN

Ye shall know the truth, and the truth shall make you free.

John 8:32

Truth is the highest thing that man may keep.

Geoffrey Chaucer

The truth is more important than the facts.

Frank Lloyd Wright

A lie can travel half way around the world while the truth is putting on its shoes.

Unknown

The only people mad at you for speaking the TRUTH are those living a lie. Keep speaking it.

Unknown

People hate the truth. Luckily, the truth doesn't care.

Unknown

The truth of the matter is that there's nothing you can't accomplish if: 1) You clearly decide what it is that you're absolutely committed to achieving, 2) You're willing to take massive actions, 3) You notice what's working or not, and 4) You continue to change your approach until you achieve what you want, using whatever life gives you along the way.

Tony Robbins

Unwavering

L ife is either a daring adventure, or it is nothing.

HELEN KELLER

W hether you think you can or think you can't, you're right.

HENRY FORD

I think I can, I think I can.

THE LITTLE ENGINE THAT COULD

I t's better to be in the arena, getting stomped by the bull, than to be up in the stands or out in the parking lot.

STEVEN PRESSFIELD

N ever give up on something that you can't go a day without thinking about.

WINSTON CHURCHILL

I n-between goals is a thing called life, that has to be lived and enjoyed.

SID CAESAR

S ometimes life hits you in the head with a brick. Don't lose faith.

STEVE JOBS

Success isn't permanent and failure isn't fatal; it's the courage to continue that counts.

UNKNOWN

As soon as anyone starts telling you to be "realistic," cross that person off your invitation list.

JOHN ELIOT

If something is important to you, you will find a way, if it isn't, you'll find an excuse.

UNKNOWN

Failure is simply the opportunity to begin again, this time more intelligently.

HENRY FORD

Win-Win

When you win, nothing hurts.

JOE NAMATH

Nobody remembers who came in second.

CHARLES M. SCHULZ

Let's win one for the Gipper.

KNUTE ROCKNE

Winning isn't everything, but wanting to win is.

VINCE LOMBARDI

*Y*our ability to be a winner 100 percent of the time is based upon giving up the notion that losing at anything is equivalent to being a loser.

DR. WAYNE W. DYER

*I*f anything goes bad, I did it. If anything goes semi-good, we did it. If anything goes really good, then you did it. That's all it takes to get people to win football games for you.

PAUL BRYANT

*T*he man who wins may have been counted out several times, but he didn't hear the referee.

H. E. JANSEN

*I*f winning isn't important, why do we spend all that money on scoreboards?

CHUCK COONRADT

*D*evelop the winning edge; small differences in your performance can lead to large differences in your results.

BRIAN TRACY

*T*o win without risk is to triumph without glory.

PIERRE CORNEILLE

*T*he act of taking the first step is what separates the winners from the losers.

BRIAN TRACY

PART V

Overtime

———◆◆◆———

When you have to make a hard decision, flip a coin. Why? Because when that coin is in the air, you suddenly know what you're hoping for.

UNKNOWN

PART VI

The Need for a Coach

——✳——

*E*veryone needs a coach. It doesn't matter whether you're a basketball player, a tennis player, a gymnast or a bridge player.

BILL GATES

I feel that a great coach is one that has a vision, sets a plan in place, has the right people in place to execute that plan and then accepts the responsibility if that plan is not carried out.

MIKE SINGLETARY

I believe in surrendering to a coach or teacher and letting that individual show me the way, instead of pursuing the route I think perfect for me.

LORAL LANGEMEIER

*I*f at first you don't succeed, try doing what your coach told you to do the first time.

UNKNOWN

*Y*ou have brains in your head. You have feet in your shoes. You can steer yourself any direction you choose. You're on your own. And you know what you know. And YOU are the one who'll decide where to go.

DR. SEUSS

A coach is someone who tells you what you do not want to hear, who has you see what you don't want to see, so you can be who you always knew you could be.

TOM LANDRY

I absolutely believe that people, unless coached, never reach their maximum capabilities.

BOB NARDELLI

*C*oaching helps you take stock of where you are now in all aspects of your life, and how that compares to where you would like to be.

ELAINE MACDONALD

*A*ll coaching is, is taking a player where he can't take himself.

BILL MCCARTNEY

*T*hey call it coaching, but it is teaching. You do not tell them it is so, but you show them the reasons why it is so, and you repeat and you repeat until they are convinced, until they know.

VINCE LOMBARDI

*L*ive life from the hash marks to the uprights!

DR. DEBORAH J. HRIVNAK

About the Author

―∽∽―

*D*r. Deborah J. Hrivnak is a professional speaker, coach, author, and the creator of the Four Step Game Plan for How to Take Action and Get Off the Sidelines and Into the "Game." She is the president and CEO of MyCoachDeborah, Inc., where she integrates her strengths-based philosophy, action-oriented approach, candor, and humor to support individuals toward greater success in their lives.

Before starting her own business, Deborah served as a special-education teacher and administrator, as well as a university professor, where she was awarded the Outstanding Teacher of the Year. A television documentary for the Nebraska State Department of Education also recognizes her notable work with learning-disabled students, and she has served on numerous committees at the district and state levels.

Deborah holds a doctorate in educational leadership and is a certified life coach. She currently resides in Saint Charles, Illinois, with her architect husband, John. Her greatest joy is spending time with their ten grandchildren, as well as watching various spectator sports—especially football. Having grown up in Nebraska, she is a devoted Husker fan. Deborah enjoys working with people and believes everyone can live life from the hash marks to the uprights!

www.ingramcontent.com/pod-product-compliance
Lightning Source LLC
Chambersburg PA
CBHW031154020426
42333CB00013B/667